BETTER SAID
AND
CLEARLY WRITTEN

BETTER SAID AND CLEARLY WRITTEN

An Annotated Guide to Business Communication Sources, Skills, and Samples

Compiled by
Sandra E. Belanger

Bibliographies and Indexes in
Mass Media and Communications, Number 3

GREENWOOD PRESS
New York • Westport, Connecticut • London

Copyright Acknowledgments

The author and publisher are grateful for permission
to reprint excerpts from the following:

Sears List of Subject Headings, 13th Edition. Copyright ©
1986, by the H.W. Wilson Company. Reproduced by permission
of the publisher.

Grammar Hotline Directory, 1989 Edition. Reprinted with the permission
of the Writing Center/Grammar Hotline, Tidewater Community
College, Virginia Beach, Virginia.

Library of Congress Cataloging-in-Publication Data

Belanger, Sandra E.
    Better said and clearly written : an annotated guide to business
communication sources, skills, and samples / compiled by Sandra E.
Belanger.
      p.   cm. — (Bibliographies and indexes in mass media and
communications, ISSN 1041-8350 ; no. 3)
    ISBN 0-313-26641-7 (lib. bdg. : alk. paper)
    1. Reference books—Business communication—Bibliography.
2. Business communication—Bibliography. 3. Business communication—
Information services—Handbooks, manuals, etc. I. Title.
II. Series.
Z7164.C81B428   1989
[HF5718]
016.6584′5—dc20   89-17227

British Library Cataloguing in Publication Data is available.

Library of Congress Catalog Card Number: 89-17227
ISBN: 0-313-26641-7
ISSN: 1041-8350

First published in 1989

Greenwood Press, Inc.
88 Post Road West, Westport, Connecticut 06881

Printed in the United States of America

The paper used in this book complies with the
Permanent Paper Standard issued by the National
Information Standards Organization (Z39.48-1984).

10 9 8 7 6 5 4 3 2 1

For My Father

Contents

PART II: Communication Skills

Chapter 4: Communication Skills   **55**

Preface

The simple request for a sample business plan precipitated a three year quest for the material contained in this guide. Road blocks, in the guise of unfriendly subject headings and tables of contents, were found and had to be overcome in the search for practical solutions to business and technical communications problems. The result is an annotated bibliography aimed primarily at business and engineering students, faculty, librarians, and other working professionals, and designed to facilitate the location of outlines, guidelines, examples, workbooks, sample documents, and similar forms of assistance. As such, it serves those who need to communicate more effectively in school and the workplace, as well as teachers and librarians who will assist them in this process.

Research began primarily with the collections of several West Coast and Midwest university and public libraries. Additional materials were gleaned from the review of reference works, indexes, cited book and periodical references, bibliographic databases in business and related fields, Dialog's LC Marc database, and the Library of Congress. All books were closely examined for their usefulness in developing communication skills among business and technical professionals. Resources listed in Chapters 2 and 3 have been verified through inspection and/or in standard reference works for the field. Unverified items have not been included. The *Grammar Hotline Directory*, updated every January, can be obtained by sending a stamped, self-addressed business envelope to: Grammar Hotline Directory, Tidewater Community College Writing Center, 1700 College Crescent, Virginia Beach, VA 23456. Bibliographic items included in Chapters 4, 5, and 6 were published primarily between 1980 and 1988, with reference made to some titles expected or published in 1989. Unless otherwise noted, all materials have been examined by the author.

This book, like many others, has benefited from the assistance of colleagues and friends. I am deeply grateful to my colleague, Robert Harmon, whose vast experience assisted this project from its inception. Many of the materials included would not have been scrutinized without the assistance of the interlibrary loan staff at San Jose State University Library: Jean Meyers, Hjordis Madsen, and Rhea Bradley. In visiting other libraries during the course of the research, I often sought the assistance of my colleagues in those institutions. I wish to thank the helpful personnel at the Hugh Jackson Business Library (Stanford University), San Jose Public Library, San Francisco Public Library,

San Francisco State University, California Polytechnic, San Luis Obispo, Milwaukee Public Library, University of Wisconsin-Milwaukee, and the Library of Congress.

Several colleagues have provided comments on the manuscript at various stages of production. As I have benefited from their assistance, I would here like to express my gratitude to Terry Crowley, Les Kong, Ron J. McBeath, Tina Brundage, Cliff Johnson, Rebecca Martin, Milton Loventhal, and Jennifer McDowell. Production of camera-ready copy could not have been completed without the guidance and assistance of Don Perrin, Instructional Resources Center, San Jose State University.

I am indebted to my friends and colleagues, especially Nancy J. Emmick and Roxanne Camp, for their continuing support and encouragement. My eternal gratitude and thanks are due to my mother, Florence Belanger, who ably assisted the research and prepared the name and title indexes.

Introduction

Both universities and employers are concerned with the ability of students and employees to communicate effectively. Communications courses emphasize the techniques of writing and the development of verbal and nonverbal skills through term papers, writing assignments, and oral presentations. The published literature is replete with concern for the communication skills of executives, managers, engineers, and others in the workplace. There is a proliferation of books offering advice and sure cures for communication problems. The business and technical worlds decry the absence of competent writing and speaking skills, yet the fast pace of the working environment diminishes the time available for learning and improving these skills. What most readily and effectively facilitates such learning for students and practitioners are clear guidelines, well-structured outlines, and pertinent examples. This book provides the locations of these essential materials and the research tools needed for their procurement.

There are two components to the bibliography. Part I consists of a research handbook, in three chapters, for conducting research in business and technical communications and answering basic questions on correct grammar. Identified are: research tools (e.g., dictionaries), research resources (e.g., indexes and computer databases) and information sources (e.g., the telephone numbers of national associations, institutions, publishers, and grammar hotlines).

Chapter 1, Research Guides, lists standard reference sources such as bibliographies, dictionaries, directories, handbooks, and sources of quotations. It identifies sources for correct definitions, biographies of important persons in the field, and quotations to use in a report or a speech. The bibliographies record previously published material in business communication and technical writing.

Chapter 2, Research Resources, expands research techniques in business and technical communication through printed indexes and abstracts, computer databases, periodicals, and library subject headings. These can be used to extend the search for articles in magazines and journals, and subsequently published books.

Chapter 3, Information Resources, covers professional associations, research institutions, government agencies, and grammar hotlines. Many professional associations, research institutions, and government agencies provide assistance with communication problems.

Part II is a guide to general, written, and oral communication skills. It consists of is a topical bibliography of books, in three chapters, offering assistance in business and technical communication. Sources in Chapters 4-6 were chosen for their emphasis on approaches, formats, checklists, guidelines, and sample documents. Books have been placed within the subject of maximum coverage, with most items appearing only once. For items where multiple editions were published between 1980 and 1989, only the most recent edition is included unless content changes mandated the addition of the older edition. Author, title, publication information, and annotation are displayed. The annotations, in describing book contents, note the presence of outlines, guidelines, sample documents, and similar items. Additional listings for multiple subject books are in the subject index. There are three indexes: name, title, and subject. Name variations appear as cross references in the name index.

Chapter 4, Communication Skills, examines books that improve general communication skills such as editing, grammar, and writing style. As proficiency in communicating affects all areas of the work environment, there is no excuse for remaining rusty. The workbooks, programmed instruction manuals, and communication overviews found in the chapter enable anyone to learn to communicate more effectively.

Books listed in Chapter 5, Written Communication, answer questions on how to write specific documents — everything from abstracts and business plans to reports and resumes. Through correspondence and more specialized written documents, management communicates with its employees, its competitors, and its customers. Misunderstandings are prevented and success guaranteed with the production of well-written materials.

Chapter 6, Oral Communication, contains works on such areas as interviewing, media relations, presentations, and public speaking. As with the written word, the ability to converse with others is a requirement for success.

PART I

Research: Guides, Resources, Information

Chapter 1

RESEARCH GUIDES

In the search for information to improve business and technical communications, there are several basic reference sources which supplement a good dictionary and thesaurus, including handy desk-top manuals and information gathering tools. This chapter is a bibliography of the standard reference sources for the communications field. Six categories are included: bibliographies, biographical sources, dictionaries, directories, handbooks, and quotation books. These sources identify correct definitions, biographies of important persons in the field, and quotations to add spice to a presentation.

Some reference tools, like bibliographies, lead to further sources; others, like dictionaries, contain the answer within the volume consulted. The presence of annotations or brief summaries in the works cited is indicated where appropriate. The biographical works give brief descriptions of an individual's life and accomplishments or reveal the location of such information. Dictionaries feature terms as defined in the field. Varying degrees of explanation are supplied for key terms, buzz words and slang expressions. A directory usually lists basic data such as name, address, telephone number and other pertinent information. The directories in this chapter index associations, periodicals, newsletters and government agencies. They can be used to modify and expand on the information found in chapters two and three. Handbooks go beyond the more limited focus of dictionaries in providing data. They offer extensive definitions, detailed examples and examine specific skills such as letter writing. The pronouncements and witticisms of experts in economics and business are often quoted in the press. To assist in their identification, pertinent collections of quotations are cited.

The basic reference sources in this chapter support the search for additional information in business and technical communications. Used appropriately, these sources will contribute to the improvement of writing and speaking skills.

BIBLIOGRAPHIES

1. Alred, Gerald J.; Reep, Diana C.; and Limaye, Mohan R. *Business and Technical Writing. An Annotated Bibliography of Books, 1880-1980*. Metuchen, NJ: Scarecrow Press, 1981. 240p.

This annotated bibliography emphasizes business and technical writing books published between 1880 and 1980. Related works covered are style guides, oral communication, language, usage and readability. The entries are arranged alphabetically with author, title and subject indexes. Indexed.

2. Bowman, Mary Ann, and Stamas, Joan D. *Written Communication in Business: A Selective Bibliography, 1967-1977*. Chicago: American Business Communication Association, 1980. 101p.

Books and periodical articles are the focus here. The subject index identifies sources of business letters, memos, reports, employee publications, resumes, direct mail, and the teaching of written communication. The alphabetical bibliography has very brief annotations. The subject index is keyed to page numbers. Items are numbered from the top of the page. Indexed.

3. Dworaczek, Marian. *Job Resume: A Bibliography*. Monticello, IL: Vance Bibliographies, 1984. 14p.

Resumes and the job search process can be investigated using this unannotated bibliography. Selected books (with some periodical articles) published between 1965 and 1983 are shown. The entries are arranged alphabetically by author. Not indexed.

4. Goldstein, Jone R., and Donovan, Robert B. *A Bibliography of Basic Texts in Technical and Scientific Writing*. Edited by David L. Carson. Washington, DC: Society for Technical Communication, 1982. 25p.

Designed for teachers, all textbooks reviewed were available as of August 1981. The alphabetical citations, with annotations, are coded by educational level. There is a separate list of additional material of interest to teachers. Not indexed.

5. Haggblade, Berle. *Business Communication*. St. Paul, MN: West Publishing, 1982. 458p.

Meant to be used as a business communications textbook, the book contains two extensive bibliographies: books by topic, and periodical articles from 1970-1980. The samples of written communication are indicated in the index. There is a separate grammar handbook. Indexed.

6. Hull, Debra L. *Business and Technical Communication: A Bibliography, 1975-1985*. Metuchen, NJ: Scarecrow Press, 1987. 229p.

This bibliography of periodical articles was created for teachers of business and technical communication. It is organized into three parts: classroom methods and programs, aspects of communication, and future areas of concern, such as computers. Each periodical reference has a content summary. Indexed.

7. Moran, Michael G., and Journet, Debra, eds. *Research in Technical Communication: A Bibliographic Sourcebook*. Westport, CT: Greenwood Press, 1985. 515p.

Each of the essays in this collection concludes with an extensive bibliography. The references provided are to both books and periodical articles. Separate guides to textbooks and style manuals are in the appendices. Indexed.

8. Mundell, Jacqueline. *Current Literature on Communication in Personnel Management, 1980-1984*. Monticello, IL: Vance Bibliographies, 1985. 10p.

Part of a series, the unannotated, selective bibliography refers to monographs and periodical articles. Each section is arranged alphabetically by author. Not indexed.

9. Society for Technical Communication. *An Annotated Bibliography on Technical Writing, Editing, Graphics and Publishing 1966-1980*. Edited by Helen V. Carlson, et al. Washington, DC: Society for Technical Communication, 1983. 661p.

This bibliography of 2700 articles and books updates the previous bibliography for 1950-1965. The topic, communicating technical information, is interpreted broadly. Those titles recently published by the Society have been added to the bibliography. There is a separate list of periodicals. Entries are arranged in numerical order necessitating use of the key word and author indexes. Indexed.

10. Vance, Mary. *Communication in Management: A Bibliography*. Monticello, IL: Vance Bibliographies, 1982. 18p.

Part of a series, most of the unannotated references are to books published from the mid 1970's to 1981. The citations are listed alphabetically by author. Not indexed.

11. Vance, Mary. *Employment Interviewing: A Bibliography*. Monticello, IL: Vance Bibliographies, 1982. 11p.

Like others from Vance Bibliographies, this one is unannotated, includes both books and periodical articles, and is arranged alphabetically by author. Most of the references are concerned with interviewing from the job hunters' point of view. Not indexed.

12. Walsh, Ruth M., and Birkin, Stanley J. *Business Communication. An Annotated Bibliography*. Westport, CT: Greenwood Press, 1980. 686p.

Designed for managers at all levels, citations to books, dissertations and periodical articles (in English) have been organized into three parts: author/title listing, key words and abstracts. The first two parts refer to the separate abstract section. The key word listing should be used to locate works on a subject. Indexed.

13. White, Jane F., and Campbell, Patty G. *Abstracts of Studies in Business Communication 1900 Through 1970*. Urbana, IL: American Business Communication Association, 1982. 272p.

Theses and dissertations in business communication, from 1900 through 1970, are given in eleven subject areas. Each topic has alphabetical citations with annotations. Newer references refer to *Dissertation Abstracts International* but do not provide the order number. Not indexed.

BIOGRAPHICAL SOURCES

14. *Biography and Genealogy Master Index*. Abr ed. Detroit, MI: Gale Research Company, 1988. 3 volumes.

First published in 1975, five-year cumulations (1981-85) and updates (1986) have appeared since the 1980 edition which had eight volumes. Biographies which appear in national, regional and specialized directories can be located with this set. Biographees are listed by last name with birth (and death) dates and code for all available biographies. It is best used for finding persons who are alive.

15. *Biography Index. A Quarterly Index to Biographical Material in Books and Magazines*. New York: H. W. Wilson, 1946-present. Monthly, Annual.

Biographical materials from periodicals, books and the other Wilson indexes are reported. For each individual, the bibliographic citation indicates where the biography appeared. There is a separate index by profession and occupation.

16. *Dictionary of Business Biography. A Biographical Dictionary of Business Leaders Active in Britain in the Period 1860-1980*. Edited by David J. Jeremy. London: Butterworths, 1984. 5 volumes.

Over one thousand biographies are furnished of British business entrepreneurs active between 1860 and 1980. Academics, civil servants, trade unionists, agriculturists and currently active business persons have been excluded. The biographies, arranged alphabetically in five volumes, have a signed essay, list of writings and bibliography of published and unpublished sources. This is best used for historical figures. Not indexed.

17. Ingham, John N. *Biographical Dictionary of American Business Leaders*. Westport, CT: Greenwood Press, 1983. 4 volumes.

Lengthy essays are offered of the most significant American business leaders active from colonial times to the present. References to other biographical sources appear at the end of an entry. The eight appendices index the biographies by industry, company, birthplace, place of activity, ethnicity, year of birth, and sex. Indexed.

18. *Reference Book of Corporate Managements. America's Corporate Leaders*. Parsippany, NJ: Dun's Marketing Services, 1988. 4 volumes.

The annual has brief biographies of corporate officers and directors. Three of the volumes are alphabetical by the company name. Within each corporate entry, educational and work histories of all the executives are given. Volume four consists of four indexes: companies alphabetically, by industry, by geographical location and by executive. Indexed.

19. *Standard and Poor's Register of Corporations, Directors and Executives*. New York: Standard and Poors, 1988. 3 volumes.

Volume 2 is an alphabetical directory of officers, directors, trustees and partners in corporations. For each executive the directory discloses business affiliation, titles, educational background, addresses and memberships. Volume 1 describes the company. There are numerous indexes in volume 3. Indexed

20. *Who's Who. An Annual Biographical Dictionary.* New York: St. Martin's Press, 1988. 1972p.

This is a biographical directory of prominent British men and women. For living persons the educational background, career highlights, publications and address are reported. The annual supplies a section on recent obituaries.

21. *Who's Who in America.* 45th ed. Wilmette, IL: Marquis Who's Who, 1988. 2 volumes.

Contemporary americans who are prominent or of widespread interest can be found in this directory. Arranged alphabetically, the entries disclose educational background, career details, awards, offices and address. Some entries have a statement, written by the person, of personal principles, goals and values. A cumulative index of retirements and deaths from previous editions is in volume two.

22. *Who's Who in Finance and Industry.* 25th ed. Chicago, IL: Marquis Who's Who, 1987. 775p.

Published biennially, the directory provides sketches of business and business-related executives, officers and management-level professionals. Entries are alphabetical and include educational background, career developments, organizational memberships and offices, and address.

23. *Who's Who in the West.* 21st ed. Wilmette, IL: Marquis Who's Who, 1987. 818p.

Individuals who live in the western U.S. and western Canada are the focus of this who's who. Arranged alphabetically by name, data such as educational background, professional positions, memberships, publications and address are shown. The companion volumes are: *Who's Who in the East, Who's Who in the Midwest,* and *Who's Who in the South and Southwest.*

24. *Who's Who of American Women.* 15th ed. Wilmette, IL: Marquis Who's Who, 1986. 903p.

Published since 1958, the directory covers women in the professions and volunteer work. Entries reveal educational background, professional positions, memberships, publications, and address.

25. *Who's Who of Emerging Leaders.* 1st ed. Wilmette, IL: Marquis Who's Who, 1987. 938p.

The focus of this directory is on new achievers identified as the emerging leaders of America.Those included usually are in their thirties and forties. Arranged alphabetically, entries give educational background, professional positions, memberships, publications and address.

DICTIONARIES AND ENCYCLOPEDIAS

26. Adam, J. H. *Longman Dictionary of Business English*. Burnt Mill, Harlow, Essex, UK: Longman; Immeuble Esseily, Place Riad South, Beirut: York Press, 1982. 492p.

Couched in easily understood English, this dictionary's definitions vary in length. A variety of business subjects are covered with examples that show words in context. Guides to metrics, measures and symbols can be found in the appendices.

27. Alexander Hamilton Institute. *A Dictionary of Business Terms*. New York: Franklin Watts, 1987. 438p.

Intended to add clarity and accuracy to business communication, over 2500 terms are defined. Terms are arranged alphabetically with brief definitions. A separate business-term locater indexes terms by their areas of business. This was previously published as *AHI's Complete Portfolio of Modern Business Terms*, and has many communications terms.

28. Bates, Jefferson D. *Writing with Precision. How to Write So That You Cannot Possibly Be Misunderstood*. rev ed. Washington, DC: Acropolis Books, 1985. 226p.

Arranged in three parts, the book has basic writing hints for anyone wanting to write plain English, particularly those in business and government. Part one contains hints, checklists and some how-to information on writing letters and reports. Part two, a dictionary, defines and describes terms and usages. Exercises and their answers form part three. Indexed.

29. Berenyi, John. *The Modern American Business Dictionary*. New York: William Morrow, 1982. 288p.

This basic dictionary considers business terms and phrases in fifty fields and disciplines. Arranged alphabetically, there are brief definitions, with a section defining slang expressions. The dictionary concludes with an essay on the historical orgins of business terms.

30. Bingham, Earl G. *Pocketbook for Technical and Professional Writers*. Belmont, CA: Wadsworth Publishing Company, 1982. 283p.

For students and professional writers, part one of the pocketbook briefly describes technical writing and style. Part two is a dictionary of topics. Constructed like an encyclopedia, the handbook highlights rules, checklists, examples, and samples of various written forms. There is a topical key to facilitate use. Indexed.

31. Connors, Tracey D. *Longman Dictionary of Mass Media and Communication*. New York: Longman, 1982. 255p.

Designed for communicators, the dictionary brings together the technical jargon and slang from different communication specialties. Terms are arranged alphabetically with definitions and indicate the area of communications for each meaning used.

32. *The Encyclopedia of Practical Business.* Edited by the Editors and Experts of Boardroom Reports. New York: Boardroom Books, 1980. 400p.

The encyclopedia investigates twenty-seven categories of information and offers practical advice, instructions and guidelines. There are brief statements with the name and address of the person from whom the information was obtained. Chapter six on executive skills considers writing, speaking and meetings. Chapter seventeen on personnel management discusses interviews. Indexed.

33. Epstein, Rachel S., and Liebman, Nina. *Biz Speak.* New York: Franklin Watts, 1986. 282p.

More than 2000 words and acronyms are defined, with an emphasis on new, humorous and slang expressions. Terms are arranged alphabetically with an indication of pronunciation and business field(s). Boldface terms within a definition identify items that are defined separately. The index by business field facilitates quick mastery of terms in that field.

34. Giordano, Albert G. *Concise Dictionary of Business Terminology.* Englewood Cliffs, NJ: Prentice-Hall, 1981. 225p.

Designed for both students and practitioners who need to improve their oral and written communication, this comprehensive dictionary explains words, abbreviations and acronyms. The abbreviations and acronyms appear in a separate section.

35. Hendrickson, Robert. *Business Talk. The Dictionary of Business Words and Phrases.* New York: Stein and Day, 1984. 251p.

This collection of colorful words and phrases pertains to the world of commerce. Not meant to be comprehensive, the dictionary includes the origin and historical context of each term.

36. Nisberg, Jay N. *The Random House Handbook of Business Terms.* New York: Random House, 1988. 303p.

Basic business terms from all areas of business are identified and defined. Designed as a guide to vocabulary for both the professional and the novice, the dictionary has brief definitions. Cross references and notes of abbreviations are given where relevant. Not indexed.

37. Oran, Daniel, and Shafritz, Jay M. *The MBA's Dictionary.* Reston, VA: Reston Publishing Company, 1983. 431p.

The vocabulary required for MBA certification is defined and discussed here with some illustrations. Basically a mini-encyclopedia for managers and students, the coverage of communication and such areas as report writing and paper preparation is excellent. Cross references appear in boldface within definitions.

38. Perry, Devern J., and Silverthorn, J. E. *Word Division Manual.* 3d ed. Cincinnati, OH: South-Western Publishing Company, 1984. 168p.

Based on a word frequency study, the 20,000 most used words in business communication are shown. Arranged alphabetically, both preferred and acceptable word divisions can be located. There are guidelines for word division. The dictionary can be used as a spelling reference.

39. Rosenberg, Jerry M. *Dictionary of Business and Management.* 2d ed. New York: John Wiley and Sons, 1983. 631p.

In this business and management dictionary, the terms are defined with some examples. Ten mathematical tables for equivalents, conversions, interest and foreign exchange are in the appendices. Programs for graduate study are listed with a summary of major business and economic events. Appendix L highlights relevant quotations with a separate subject index.

40.   Selden, William, and Nanassy, Louis C.   *The Business Dictionary.* Englewood Cliffs, NJ: Prentice-Hall, 1984. 218p.

The simple, alphabetical list of business terms includes communications terms are included. The definitions vary in length. Twelve appendices comprise a handbook of abbreviations, letter and memo formats, proofreading aids and typewriting measurements.

41.   Swindle, Robert E., and Swindle, Elizabeth M.   *A to Z Business Office Handbook.* Englewood Cliffs, NJ: Prentice-Hall, 1984. 335p.

Both a dictionary and a handbook, words are arranged alphabetically with cross-references.   Some of the definitions are quite extensive, and have examples of usage or sample forms.   Other samples of an agenda, report, proposal and memo can be found within the context of their definitions. Forms of address are at the back of the book. Indexed.

DIRECTORIES

42. *Encyclopedia of Associations.* 23rd ed.   Edited by Karin E. Koek, Susan B. Martin and Annette Novallo. Detroit, MI: Gale Research, 1989. 4 volumes.

Since 1956, this directory has comprehensively listed American organizations. Currently over twenty thousand trade, professional, fraternal, union and other organizations are grouped by subject. Entries contain name, address, telephone number, president, founding date, number of members and a statement of purpose.   The index volume provides key words and association names alphabetically.   A companion set, *Encyclopedia of Associations International Organizations* has similar information for international associations. Indexed.

43. *Federal Yellow Book. A Directory of the Federal Departments and Agencies.* New York; Washington, DC: Monitor Publishing Company, 1988. 698p.

This directory focuses on U. S. Government agencies, subagencies and bureaus. Names and telephone numbers of officials are given. The listing for each agency is quite detailed. Indexed.

44. *Gale Directory of Publications.* Detroit, MI: Gale Research Company, 1988. 2 volumes.

Formerly entitled *Ayer Directory of Publications*, it indexes newspapers, journals and other trade publications annually. Arranged geographically for the U.S. and

Canada, entries report address, telephone number, details of frequency, format, subscription and advertising. Indexed.

45. *Guide to Special Issues and Indexes of Periodicals.* 3d ed. Edited by Miriam Uhlan. New York: Special Libraries Association, 1985. 160p.

Arranged by journal name, the production of special issues is identified. For each, the month issued and the price are indicated. It can be used to locate lists of advertisers, buyers guides, directory issues, statistical features and such items as the Fortune 500. Indexed.

46. *Newsletters Directory.* 3d ed. Edited by Brigitte T. Darnay and John Nimchuk. Detroit, MI: Gale Research Company, 1987. 1162p.

This is a directory of over eight thousand newsletters published and available in the United States. Several sections pertain to business and communications. The directory reveals publication and subscription details, content, intended audience and editorial policies. Indexed.

47. *Oxbridge Directory of Newsletters.* 6th ed. New York: Oxbridge Communications, 1988. 544p.

Fifteen thousand newsletters in over one hundred categories are indexed in this comprehensive work. In each category, the publisher, newsletter's address, physical characteristics, key personnel, purpose, cost and inclusion of advertising are cited. While there is no category specifically for communication, relevant newsletters can be located in the management and journalism sections. Indexed.

48. *Serials Directory: An International Reference Book.* 2d ed. Birmingham, AL: Ebsco Publishing, 1987. 3 volumes.

Journals and other serial publications are listed by subject. For each periodical, the directory discloses its date of publication, language, frequency, price, telephone number and editor. Designations have been added indicating where it is indexed and the inclusion of book reviews and advertising. Volume 3 has alphabetical title and ceased title indexes. Indexed.

49. *Special Issues Index. Specialized Contents of Business, Industrial, and Consumer Journals.* Compiled by Robert Sicignano and Doris Prichard. Westport, CT: Greenwood Press, 1982. 309p.

The English language journals and trade magazines listed here produce specialized issues and indexes as part of their publications. For each title, the special issues are reported in chronological order, with address and price indicated. Indexed.

50. *Standard Periodicals Directory.* 11th ed. New York: Oxbridge Communications, 1988. 1594p.

A comprehensive directory of U. S. and Canadian periodicals, the directory is organized by subject. Within each subject, journal entries give name, publisher, address, phone number, circulation and advertising data. There is a cross index to subjects. Indexed.

51. *Standard Rate and Data Service: Business Publication Rates and Data*. Skokie, IL: Standard Rate and Data Service, monthly. 3 volumes.

In order by industry, this directory of trade journals presents publisher, editorial profile, personnel data and advertising rates. Part two has rates for the classified sections of trade publications. Part three shows direct-response and international journals. Indexed.

52. *Ulrich's International Periodicals Directory*. 27th ed. New York: R. R. Bowker, 1988. 3 volumes

Within each subject category, U. S. and foreign journals are presented alphabetically. For each title the publisher, frequency, address, circulation, and other available data (where indexed, format, and title changes) are supplied. Volume three lists ceased titles and publications of international organizations. Indexed.

53. *United States Government Manual*. Washington, DC: Government Printing Office, 1988. 891p.

The annual directory explains U.S. government agencies, boards, committees and commissions for all three branches of government. Besides address and phone numbers, it describes the agency, showing duties, how established, regional organization and primary personnel. The quasi-official agencies are also identified. Indexed.

HANDBOOKS

54. Anastasi, Thomas E. Jr. *Desk Guide to Communication*. 2d ed. Boston: CBI Publishing Company, 1981. 285p.

This is a two-part handbook which provides for skill development in a reference format. Part I consists of seventeen chapters of practical guidance on grammar, punctuation and preparation of written and oral communications. Part II is an alphabetical guide to usage, grammar, punctuation, spelling, pronunciation and general information. Letter formats are in the appendix. Indexed.

55. Barnum, Carol M. *Prose and Cons. The Do's and Don'ts of Technical and Business Writing*. Elmsford, NY: National Publishers, 1986. 156p.

A reference guide for students and beginners, Barnum's book can be used to develop an appropriate prose writing style. General rules, grammar, editing, and punctuation are cited. Practical advice on knowing your audience, writing a summary, and creating graphics is contained in this handbook, along with an exercise section. Indexed.

56. Bittleston, John, and Shorter, Barbara. *The Book of Business Communications Checklists*. New York: John Wiley and Sons, 1982. 166p.

The handbook is a compilation of forty-one checklists in business communication. Using an outline approach, the key elements and decisions described are aimed at specific written documents, oral communication situations and the audiences addressed. The authors convey the fundamental rules of good communication with guidelines. Blank checklists appear in the back. Indexed.

57. Bovee, Courtland L., and Thill, John V. *Business Communication Today*. New York: Random House, 1986. 650p.

Examples from real companies are used for skill development in the business world. Thirty-two checklists and models pepper the discussion of letters, memos, proposals, reports, interviews, meetings and presentations. Special feature boxes report contemporary issues. The text also treats grammar and usage. A new edition is to be published in 1989. Indexed.

58. Brusaw, Charles T.; Alred, Gerald J.; and Oliu, Walter E. *The Business Writer's Handbook*. 3d ed. New York: St. Martin's Press, 1987. 764p.

This is a comprehensive, desk-top reference for students and business professionals. Writing problems are solved through definition, examples, and the inclusion of representative samples. Terms can be located through the index, the checklist of the writing process, or the topical key to the alphabetical entries. The third edition does not include the bibliography of related sources that was in the second edition. Indexed.

59. Brusaw, Charles T.; Alred, Gerald J.; and Oliu, Walter E. *Handbook of Technical Writing*. 2d ed. New York: St. Martin's Press, 1982. 697p.

Like the authors similar handbook for business, this desk-top reference is concerned with solutions to technical writing problems. Subjects are alphabetical with an index, writing process checklist, and topical key. Grammar and punctuation are considered. There are samples of specific technical writing forms. While this volume does overlap with the business handbook, some of the topics and many of the examples are unique. Indexed.

60. Clark, James L., and Clark, Lyn R. *How 3: A Handbook for Office Workers*. Boston: Kent Publishing Company, 1982. 297p.

In the handbook, the preparation of written documents by office workers is emphasized. Grammar and usage are debated along with specific forms such as letters, memos and reports. There are examples and guidelines. The solution finder in each chapter and the shortcuts in the appendix are valuable. A new edition entitled *How 5: A Handbook for Office Workers should be available in 1988. Indexed*.

61. DiGaetani, John L., ed. *The Handbook of Executive Communication*. Homewood, IL: Dow Jones-Irwin, 1986. 894p.

Sixty-four essays in eight subject sections analyze such aspects of executive communication as annual reports, newsletters and successful speaking. The essays, which were written by communications specialists, bring together different points of view, pertinent illustrations and examples. Indexed.

62. Doris, Lillian, and Miller, Besse M. *Complete Secretary's Handbook*. 6th ed. Revised by Mary A. DeVries. Englewood Cliffs, NJ: Prentice-Hall, 1988. 664p.

Writing principles and secretarial techniques are combined with the use of new technology. Writing skills, grammar and punctuation are studied with guidelines and samples of letters and memos. Advice is offered for preparing reports and word processing. There is a handy reference guide to abbreviations, symbols, measures and glossary. Indexed.

63. Gootnick, David E., and Gootnick, Margaret M., eds. *The Standard Handbook of Business Communication*. New York: Free Press, 1984. 479p.

Designed for students and educators, twenty-seven articles have been organized into five divisions: career planning, written communication, interactional communication, organizational communication, and foundations and frontiers. A source of instructional methods and strategies, some essays address specific writing problems such as letters or reports. Indexed.

64. House, Clifford R., and Sigler, Kathie. *Reference Manual for the Office*. 7th ed. Cincinnati, OH: Southwestern Publishing Company, 1989. 343p.

Volume unavailable for examination.

65. Pearlman, Daniel D., and DuBose, Anita. *Letter Perfect: An ABC for Business Writers*. Indianapolis, IN: Bobbs-Merrill, 1985. 96p.

The essentials of style, usage and mechanics are treated, emphasizing the revision process. Arranged by correction symbol, definitions, how-to explanations and examples are advanced. The handbook stresses editing problems with diagnostic charts in the back. Not indexed.

66. Quinn, Michelle. *Katharine Gibbs Handbook of Business English*. New York: Free Press; London: Collier Macmillan, 1982. 275p.

A basic handbook of grammar and usage for business students, punctuation, sentences and related areas are investigated. This serves as a companion guide to *Katharine Gibbs Business Wordbook*. The handbook contains model business letters and how to write them. There is a glossary and a reference section on abbreviations and proofreading. Indexed.

67. Rogoff, Leonard; Ballenger, Grady; and Faherty, Victoria B. *Office Guide to Business Letters, Memos and Reports*. New York: Arco Publishing, 1984. 249p.

Business correspondence is presented in a basic handbook. The volume is comprised of advice, checklists and samples of letters, memos, newsletters and reports. Additional sections embrace style, punctuation and abbreviations. There is a glossary. Not Indexed.

68. Scala, Bea, and Nicholson, Joan. *Katharine Gibbs Business Wordbook*. New York: Free Press; London: Collier Macmillan, 1982. 358p.

The wordbook is a comprehensive guide to spelling. A sizable glossary and a reference section on usage, abbreviations and related topics are provided. It serves as a companion volume to *Katharine Gibbs Handbook of Business English*. Not indexed.

69. Warner, Joan E. *Business English Handbook*. Reston, VA: Reston Publishing Company, 1982. 271p.

Primarily concerned with grammar, punctuation and style, the handbook considers how these are used to create clarity in business writing. The examples used are from business situations. Abbreviations, forms of address and other topics can be found in a separate reference section. This volume is useful to anyone needing a review of English usage. Indexed.

70. Whalen, Doris H. *Handbook of Business English*. New York: Harcourt Brace Jovanovich, 1980. 264p.

In this English usage reference manual, readers are acquainted with sentences, parts of speech, punctuation, style, spelling, and word usage. The numerous examples contribute to the book's usefulness in checking rules of grammar and usage. A section of seventy-five self-checking exercises support use as a textbook or self-study manual. Indexed.

71. Whalen, Doris H. *The Secretary's Handbook: A Manual for Office Personnel*. 4th ed. New York: HBJ Media Systems; Harcourt Brace Jovanovich, 1983. 326p.

Acceptable office and language skills are presented, such as office procedures, grammar, punctuation, style and usage. Model letters and memos can be found in chapter two. There are sixty exercises with an answer key. Forms of address, proofreaders marks, abbreviations, reference sources and a glossary appear in the appendix. Indexed.

QUOTATIONS

72. Charlton, James, ed. *The Executive's Quotation Book*. New York: St. Martin's Press, 1983. 86p.

This is a selection of over four hundred quotations about money, work and related subjects. A name index is included but the lack of a subject index or a table of contents make it difficult to use. Not indexed.

73. Hay, Peter. *The Book of Business Anecdotes*. New York: Facts on File, 1988. 296p.

Anecdotes, with quotations, have been collected in twelve subject categories such as money, selling, corporate culture and politics. Intended to entertain and inspire, it highlights both general business ancecdotes and those of professional interest. Indexed.

74. Iapoce, Michael. *A Funny Thing Happened on the Way to the Boardroom. Using Humor in Business Speaking*. New York: John Wiley and Sons, 1988. 205p.

Basic instruction is offered in the use of humor in business presentations, with helpful hints and examples. Part two consists of jokes, one liners and stories to make a point. The jokes can be located through the table of contents and the index. Indexed.

75. Jackman, Michael, ed. *The Macmillan Book of Business and Economic Quotations*. New York: Macmillan, 1984. 302p.

This book of quotations traces the economic thought of man within sixty-two subject areas. Designed as a survival tool, there are many quotations from the 1980's. Quotations are arranged chronologically in each subject with separate biographical, source and key word indexes. Indexed.

76. James, Simon, comp. *A Dictionary of Economic Quotations*. London: Croom Helm, 1981. 244p.

Economics quotations, with few from contemporary writers, are grouped into 133 topics. Each entry indicates the author and the work from which the quotation was taken. Indexed.

77. Simmons, S. H. *How to be the Life of the Podium.* New York: AMACOM, 1982. 294p.

Briefly presents practical advice about writing a speech. Then offers quotes, collected and written by the author, with which to enliven a speech. Has both biographical and subject indexes. Indexed.

78. White, Rolf B., comp. *The Great Business Quotations.* Secaucus, NJ: Lyle Stuart, 1986. 271p.

This collection has mostly modern quotations, sayings and wisecracks in fourteen sections. It is full of hints and useful tips. Section eleven on communication covers reading, books, speeches, public speaking, and bores. Indexed.

Chapter 2

RESEARCH RESOURCES

A thorough subject search involves locating both books and journal articles. The bibliographies in the previous chapter will not lead to new developments in business and technical communications. These can only be discovered through a search of periodical indexes, bibliographic databases, newly published books, and recent issues of journals and newsletters in the field. This chapter identifies four resources for the information search: indexes and abstracts, computer databases, journals and newsletters, and the library subject headings necessary to access collections in academic and public libraries.

Most libraries subscribe to journals, indexes, and bibliographic databases. In printed indexes, journal articles and other reports are classified, usually by subject. Some indexes can be searched also by author, title and numerical code. The indexes listed in this chapter retrieve references to those journal articles which offer guidelines, promote preferred techniques and provide sample documents.

In the last few years several indexes have been released in compact disc (CD/ROM) format. CD/ROM databases offer search capabilities similar to online bibliographic databases, with a greater ability to control costs. Two primary advantages to researching a topic with an online or CD database are: (1) the ability to combine the separate concepts in a unique fashion and, (2) the speed at which it can be done. While all printed indexes retrieve citations to magazine articles and journal papers, some databases contain the complete text of written reports, numerical tables or proprietary research.

Contained in this chapter are the addresses and telephone numbers of the major printed indexes, database vendors, and bibliographic and directory databases. The bibliographic databases provide access to journals, newspapers, government publications, dissertations and related studies. While a large number of journals and newspapers are published each year, only the most relevant titles are listed here. For each journal and newsletter the telephone number, publisher, dates, and contents are reported.

Libraries usually organize their collections by subject. Universities employ the Library of Congress Classification System and public libraries the Dewey Decimal System. Access to a library's collections is obtained by using its catalog, whether printed cards, microform format or online public access catalog. All systems use subject headings (albeit different ones) to identify relevant books.

The subject headings best used for business and technical communications books are listed here: *Sears List of Subject Headings* for public libraries and *Library of Congress Subject Headings* for academic and corporate libraries.

ABSTRACTS AND INDEXES

79. *ABI/INFORM Ondisc.* Ann Arbor, MI: University Microfilms International, 1984-present. (313-761-4700)

Over eight hundred business journals are abstracted in subjects from accounting to taxation. Business and technical communications materials are displayed extensively. This is the compact disc equivalent to the business database of the same name. A major advantage is that it can be searched in the same manner as an online database but without the cost per use.

80. *Applied Science and Technology Index.* New York: H.W. Wilson, 1958-present. (212-588-8400)

Published from 1913-1957 under the title *Industrial Arts Index,* the index focuses on journals in engineering, technology, and the applied sciences. The index contains articles from technical writing journals. It is available as an onlinr or compact disc database through Wilsonline and in compact disc format.

81. *British Education Index.* Leeds, England: Education Library, University of Leeds, 1961-present.

This source selectively examines over three hundred British periodicals by subject. The articles in education periodicals consider communication skills and their application in the workplace.

82. *Business Periodicals Index.* New York: H. W. Wilson, 1958-present. (212-588-8400)

The best known index for overall coverage of business periodicals, it provides subject access to all topic areas. Published from 1913-1957 under the title *Industrial Arts Index,* the index is also a computer database (Wilsonline) and in compact disc format. Some of the business communication journals and articles reported address the application of communications techniques in the workplace.

83. *Canadian Business Index.* Toronto: Micromedia Limited, 1975-present. (416-593-5211)

Canadian business periodicals and newspapers (*Financial Post, Financial Times,* and the *Globe and Mail*) are indexed. Research is supported in such fields as administration, industry and economics.

84. *CIS Index. Index to Publications of the United States Congress.* Washington, DC: Congressional Information Service, 1970-present. (301-654-1550)

Congressional hearings, meetings, reports and studies can be accessed by subject, title, and item number (bill, report, document, hearing, and print numbers). The companion volume contains abstracts of each publication cited. It is useful for locating government studies and identifying experts.

85. *Communication Abstracts*. Beverly Hills, CA: Sage Publications, 1978-present. (805-499-0721)

This is a comprehensive index, with abstracts, to communication journals and books. Areas examined are communication theory, interpersonal communication, small groups and organizational communications. Arranged topically, with subject and author indexes, it is a most useful source for business communication and technical writing materials.

86. *Current Index to Journals in Education*. Phoenix, AZ: Oryx Press, 1966-present. (602-254-6156)

Over seven hundred education and education-related journals are abstracted. Part of the ERIC system (Educational Resources Information Center), it has a topical arrangement and uses a controlled vocabulary. Each reference to a journal article has a content abstract. Its companion series is *Resources in Education*. Both are available in online database and compact disc formats. Among the subjects reported are business communication, technical writing, and business education.

87. *Current Technology Index*. London: Library Association; Phoenix, AZ: Oryx Press, 1981-present. (602-254-6156)

Engineering, chemical technology, manufacturing, and the pure sciences are reviewed. Four hundred British technical journals are indexed in a subject arrangement, with an author index.

88. *Education Index*. New York: H. W. Wilson, 1929-present. (212-588-8400)

This is an author/subject index to education periodicals. Pertinent business communication and technical writing journals are cited. The material is available as a computer database (Wilsonline) and in compact disc format.

89. *Engineering Index*. New York: Engineering Information, 1982-present. (212-705-7615)

Technical literature in all areas of engineering is examined. Citations to journal articles are organized by subject, with a separate listing of terms and an author index. It is available as a computer database, *Compendex*.

90. *General Periodicals Index*. San Mateo, CA: Information Access Corporation, 1983-present. (800-227-8431)

Part of the Infotrac compact disc system, the index combines parts of the *Magazine Index* and the *Business Index*. The academic edition includes all of the business journals and part of the general magazines while the public library edition does the reverse. The academic edition examines the areas of business communication and technical writing. The compact disc format allows for quick searching and printing of the results.

91. *Humanities Index*. New York: H. W. Wilson, 1974-present. (212-588-8400)

English language journals are surveyed in the fields of archaeology, area studies, folklore, history, language and literature, performing arts, philosophy, religion and theology. Articles on language and language studies are reported. This index, which is arranged by subject and author, is also available as an online database (Wilsonline) and in compact disc format. It was part of the *Social Sciences and Humanities Index* until 1974 and the *International Index* from 1905-1965.

92. *Monthly Catalog of United States Government Publications*. Washington, DC: Government Printing Office, 1895-present. (202-783-3238)

This is a monthly index to all publications of the U.S. government. Publications of all departments, bureaus and the Congress are considered with indexes by author, title, subject, keyword and number (series, report, contract and stock numbers). The standard bibliographic information is given along with the document's availability for sale.

93. *Personnel Literature*. Washington, DC: Office of Personnel Management Library, 1979-present. (202-738-3238)

The books, journal articles and government publications received by the U. S. Office of Personnel Management Library are related here. Using general personnel management subjects, it continues an index published from 1941-1978 by the U. S. Civil Service Commission Library.

94. *Personnel Management Abstracts*. Chelsea, MI: Personnel Management Abstracts, 1955-present. (313-475-1979)

Management and organizational behavior articles in academic and trade journals are considered. A broad subject arrangement is used. Content abstracts accompany each bibliographic citation.

95. *Psychological Abstracts*. Washington, DC: American Psychological Association, 1927-present. (202-833-7600)

Journal articles, books, dissertations and other technical documents are indexed in a monthly annotated bibliography. A controlled vocabulary is used. Each issue has brief subject and author indexes, which are cumulated by volume. The articles from a number of communications and organizational behavior journals are cited in this source. It is available as an online database and in compact disc format.

96. *Public Affairs Information Service Bulletin*. New York: Public Affairs Information Service, 1915-present. (212-736-6629)

Those journals, books and government publications which emphasize economic and social conditions, public administration and international relations are considered. Numerous managment and organizational communications articles, particularly in an international context, can be located with this index. A subject arrangement is employed with annual cumulations and an author index.

97. *Resources in Education*. Washington, DC: U. S. Department of Education; Phoenix, AZ: Oryx Press, 1975-present. (202-254-5500)

Part of the ERIC system, reports and other unpublished material are indexed, each with a consecutively arranged number (ED) and abstract. Each issue of the index includes a subject index, using a controlled vocabulary, and an author index. This is an excellent source for communications, business communication and technical writing materials. Libraries which subscribe receive the accompanying reports on microfiche.

98. *Science Citation Index.* Philadelphia, PA: Institute for Scientific Information, 1961-present. (215-386-0100)

Scientific and technical literature is organized by key word, author and cited reference. Author and cited reference volumes refer to the source volumes which display the journal citation. The permuterm subject volumes are very useful for searching buzz words. The index also appears as a database and in compact disc format.

99. *Social Science Citation Index.* Philadelphia, PA: Institute for Scientific Information, 1973-present. (215-386-0100)

Similar to the *Science Citation Index* but, in indexing the social sciences, contains more of the business communications and organizational communications literature. It functions in the same manner with identical format options.

100. *Social Sciences Index.* New York: H. W. Wilson, 1974-present. (212-588-8400)

Major journals in the social sciences (anthropology, economics, geography, international relations, criminology, policy sciences, political science, psychology, and related areas) are indexed by subject and author. Management and organizational communications literature are an important component. It formed part of the *Social Sciences and Humanities Index* prior to 1974 and the *International Index* from 1905-1965.

101. *Work Related Abstracts.* Detroit, MI: Information Coordinators, 1973-present. (313-962-9720)

Periodical articles and dissertations are indexed by subject. Citations are in chronological order, with reference made to that number from the index. Each listing has the necessary publication information and a brief abstract. Such areas as employee communications, union-related issues, organizational communications and related communications issues are studied in detail.

COMPUTER DATABASES

Databases are produced by vendors much in the same manner as an index to periodical articles or a reference directory is created. In order be accessed, one has to subscribe to the vendor which handles the product (or database). Listed here are the major vendors and databases most relevant for business and technical communications questions. Many public, academic and company libraries subscribe to one or more systems and provide computer literature searches for their clientele (some through payment of a fee).

Database Vendors

102. BRS Information Technologies (BRS). 1200 Route 7, Latham, NY 12110. (800-345-4BRS) (Also produces BRS Afterdark)

103. Dialog Information Services (DIALOG). 3460 Hillview Ave., Palo Alto, CA 94304. (800-334-2564, 415-858-3719) (Also produces Knowledge Index)

104. Mead Data Central (MEAD). P. O. Box 933, Dayton, OH 45401. (800-227-9597, 800-227-8379 in Ohio)

105. SDC Information Services (SDC). 2500 Colorado Ave., Santa Monica, CA 90406. (800-421-7229)

106. Vu/TEXT Information Services (VUTEXT). 1211 Chestnut St., Philadelphia, PA 19107. (800-258-8080)

107. Wilsonline (WILSON). H. W. Wilson, 950 University Ave., Bronx, NY 10452. (800-622-4002) (Also produces databases on cd/rom)

Databases

108. *ABI/Inform.* Louisville, KY: Data Courier, 1971-present. (BRS, DIALOG, MEAD, VUTEXT, SDC)

All areas of management and the decision sciences are investigated. Entries include extensive abstract of the article's contents. It refers to journal articles in business subjects from accounting through taxation, with excellent coverage of business and technical communications. Substantive abstracts accompany each journal reference. While expensive to use, it is worth the cost. It is now available also in compact disc format from University Microfilms International.

109. *Applied Science and Technology Index.* New York: H. W. Wilson, 1983-present. (WILSON)

This is a database compiled from over three hundred English-language journals in the applied sciences and technology. Articles about technical writing and the production of technical manuals are cited. The database corresponds to the print source of the same name.

110. *Biography Index.* New York: H. W. Wilson, 1984-present. (WILSON)

Biographies which appear in both periodicals and books (collective and individual biographies) form the database. The printed version is retrospective to the 1930's.

111. *Biography Master Index.* Detroit, MI: Gale Research Company, 1981-present. (DIALOG)

The current and historical biographies which appear in several hundred specialized who's whos comprise this source. Like the hardcover publication, *Biography and Genealogy Master Index,* it refers to the source directories in which the biography appears.

112. *Business Periodicals Index.* New York: H. W. Wilson, 1982-present. (WILSON)

Similar to its print equivalent, the database presents major journals from all areas of business. For years the standard source for journal articles in business, business communication and related topics are covered extensively.

113. *CIS*. Washington, DC: Congressional Information Service, 1970-present. (DIALOG)

Like the printed index by the same name, all publications of the U.S. Congress are reported. It supports searches by report and bill number as well as subject.

114. *Compendex*. New York: Engineering Information, 1970-present. (BRS, DIALOG, SDC)

The database, in corresponding to *Engineering Index*, examines all areas of engineering. There are abstracts of journal articles and conference papers. Among the topics covered is technical writing.

115. *Education Index*. New York: H. W. Wilson, 1983-present. (WILSON)

In tracking business and technical education, this database indexes articles on various aspects of professional communication such as writing, interviews, resumes, and oral communication. The database also appears in a printed version.

116. *Educational Resources Information Center*. National Institute of Education, 1966-present. (BRS, DIALOG, SDC)

The ERIC database combines two print sources: *Resources in Education* (RIE) and *Current Index to Journals in Education* (CIJE). Both journals and unpublished material in education (and related fields) are abstracted. The system supports the search for business and technical communication articles.

117. *Encyclopedia of Associations*. Detroit, MI: Gale Research Company, Annual edition. (DIALOG)

Just like its printed equivalent, the encyclopedia is comprised of information on several thousand trade associations, societies, unions and other organizations. The purpose of the organization and its publications are disclosed in a brief abstract.

118. *GPO Monthly Catalog*. Washington, DC: U. S. Government Printing Office, 1976-present. (BRS, DIALOG)

As the database version of *Monthly Catalog of United States Government Publications*, it indexes a wealth of publications from federal agencies. Reports related to business and technical communication from a government perspective can be found here.

119. *Humanities Index*. New York: H. W. Wilson, 1984-present. (WILSON)

In covering the general subject fields of the humanities, journals on language and usage are studied. The database accesses the same publications as the printed index.

120. *Inspec*. London: The Institution of Electrical Engineers, 1969-present. (BRS, DIALOG, SDC)

The database combines several printed indexes into one source. Some of the periodicals with articles about technical communications problems appear here.

121. *Linguistics and Language Behavior Abstracts*. San Diego, CA: Sociological Abstracts, 1973-present. (DIALOG)

Answers questions pertaining to interpersonal communications, nonverbal communications, speech and the nature and use of language. Summaries of articles are offered with full bibliographic data.

122. *Magazine Index*. Belmont, CA: Information Access, 1959-70, 1973-present. (BRS, DIALOG)

General interest journals are investigated, with extensive coverage of current affairs. There is a companion database which contains the full text of articles for over one hundred magazines.

123. *Management Contents*. Belmont, CA: Information Access, 1974-present. (BRS, DIALOG, SDC)

Research is reported for management and related topics such as organizational behavior. Useful abstracts accompany the journal citation. Business communications problems are addressed by the periodicals indexed in this source.

124. *MLA International Bibliography*. New York: H. W. Wilson, 1981-present. (WILSON)

Journals and other documents on language, linguistics and literature are studied. Communication in its treatment of human and invented languages is stressed.

125. *National Newspaper Index*. Belmont, CA: Information Access Company, 1979-present. (BRS, DIALOG)

Five newspapers are covered: *Wall Street Journal*, *New York Times*, *Christian Science Monitor*, *Washington Post* and *Los Angeles Times* (the last two since 1982). There is extensive concentration on communication as related to business, journalism and public relations.

126. *Newsearch*. Belmont, CA: Information Access, current month only. (BRS, DIALOG)

This is a good source for communications news as related to specific recent events or companies. News stories, articles and regional business publications are cited for the current month. The references are then transferred to other subject oriented databases by the same producer.

127. *Newspaper Abstracts*. Ann Arbor, MI: University Microfilms, 1984-present. (DIALOG)

Articles from over twenty major newspapers are provided. Summaries of each article are available.

128. *Newspaper Index*. Wooster, OH: Bell and Howell, 1976-present. (SDC)

Local, regional, state and national events are reported in this database. Newspapers, such as the twenty national newspapers indexed here, often debate the communications concerns of professionals and employees.

129. *Nexis*. Dayton, OH: Mead Data Central, 1975-present. (MEAD)

The full text is offered of stories from general and business newspapers, magazines and other information services. Rather than citing the appearance of a story, this database provides the complete written version.

130. *PAIS International*. New York: Public Affairs Information Service, 1972-present. (BRS, DIALOG)

Similar to the printed index, the computerized version accesses the public policy literature of business, economics, government and the social sciences. Communications and organization communications are examined from an international perspective.

131. *PTS Prompt*. Cleveland, OH: Predicasts, 1972-present. (BRS, DIALOG, VUTEXT)

Marketing and corporate information is emphasized. Major articles are mentioned with abstracts. Some business and technical communication materials are included, particularly those related to corporate practice.

132. *PsychInfo*. Washington, DC: American Psychological Association, 1967-present. (BRS, DIALOG, SDC)

Organizational communication and various aspects of business and interpersonal communication are stressed. In embracing research studies in interpersonal communication, it corresponds to *Pyschological Abstracts*.

133. *SciSearch*. Philadelphia, PA: Institute for Scientific Information, 1974-present. (DIALOG)

In covering science and technology literature, some technical writing and related articles are offered. The database contains the bibliographies of the articles indexed. These can be searched to track cited references to important older articles.

134. *Social SciSearch*. Philadelphia, PA: Institute for Scientific Information, 1972-present. (BRS, DIALOG, SDC)

The database investigates every area of the social and behavioral sciences. Some organizational and interpersonal communication articles are indexed. Like the science equivalent, it is useful for finding cited references.

135. *Social Sciences Index*. New York: H. W. Wilson, 1983-present. (WILSON)

All areas of the social sciences are considered with extensive examination of business, politics and foreign affairs. This is a valuable choice for research articles in business, organizational and interpersonal communication.

136. *Ulrich's International Periodicals Directory*. New York: R. R. Bowker, Current. (BRS, DIALOG)

This is the standard directory for researching data about magazines and journals in all subject areas. The database examines all journals and newsletters in a field.

LIBRARY SUBJECT HEADINGS

137. *Library of Congress Subject Headings*. 11th ed. Washington, DC: Library of Congress, 1988. 3 volumes.

Administrative Manuals
Applications for Positions
Business—Dictionaries
Business—Quotations
Business Communication
Business Consultants
Business Literature—Publishing—Data Processing
Business Report Writing
Business Writing
Commerce—Dictionaries
Commercial Correspondence
Committees
Communication in Management
Communication in Organizations
Communication in Personnel Management
Communication in Public Administration
Communication of Technical Information
Computers—Handbooks, Manuals, etc.
Corporate Meetings
Corporate Planning (for business plans)
Economics—Quotations
Economics—Research—Handbooks
Editing
Electronic Data Processing Documentation
Employee Selection
Employees' Magazines, Handbooks, etc.
Employment Interviewing
English Language—Business English
English Language—Rhetoric
English Language—Technical English
Entrepreneur (for business plans)
Executives
Executives—Language
Exposition (Rhetoric)
Government Report Writing
House Organs
Interpersonal Communication
Interviewing
Interviewing in Television
Leadership
Letter-writing
Listening
Meetings
Memorandums

New Business Enterprises—Planning (for business
plans)
Newsletters
Oral Communication
Organizational Behavior
Personnel Management
Persuasion (Rhetoric)
Proposal Writing in Business
Proposal Writing in the Social Sciences
Prospectus Writing
Public Relations
Public Speaking
Quotations
Report Writing
Resumes (Employment)
Seminars
Small Business—Finance (for business plans)
Small Business—Planning (for business plans)
Technical Correspondence
Technical Literature
Technical Manuals
Technical Writing
Venture Capital (for business plans)

138. *Sears List of Subject Headings.* 13th ed. Edited by Carmen Rovira and
Caroline Reyes. New York: H. W. Wilson, 1986. 681p.

Applications for Positions
Authorship
Business—Bibliography
Business—Handbook
Business—Indexes
Business—Periodicals
Business Letters
Commerce—
Communication
Computers—
Congresses and Conventions
Economics—
Encyclopedias and Dictionaries
English language—Business English
English language—Dictionaries
Entrepreneurs
Interviewing
Journalism (for editing)
Leadership
Lectures and Lecturing
Letter Writing
Listening
Nonverbal Communication

> Personnel Management
> Public Meetings
> Public Relations
> Public Speaking
> Publishers and Publishing (for editing)
> Quotations
> Report Writing
> Resumes (Employment)
> Rhetoric
> Small Business
> Technical Writing
> Technology—Language
> Writing

PERIODICALS AND NEWSLETTERS

139. *American Society of Business Press Editors News*. North Olmstead, OH: American Society of Business Press Editors, Bimonthly. (216-531-8306)

Provided free to members of the association, this newsletter is aimed at editors of business, trade and technical publications.

140. *Associated Business Writers of America Confidential Bulletin*. Aurora, CO: Associated Business Writers of America, Monthly. (303-751-7844)

Affiliated with the National Writers Club, the association's newsletter ensures a means of communication between members, most of whom are freelance business writers.

141. *Bulletin of the Association for Business Communicators*. Urbana, IL: Association for Business Communication, University of Illinois, Quarterly. (217-333-1006)

Entitled *ABCA Bulletin* prior to 1985, the journal contains practical articles on business communication for teachers and practitioners. The emphasis is on teaching and training.

142. *Business and the Media*. Washington, DC: Media Institute, Three times per year. (202-298-7512)

This newsletter describes news of the Institute, research in the field and available publications, both paper and videotape formats. Business/media relations, new technologies and communication issues are the focus of Institute research and programs.

143. *College Composition and Communication*. Urbana, IL: National Council of Teachers of English, Four times per year. (212-960-8759)

Publishes research-based articles on the theory, practice, history, politics and teaching of composition. The refereed journal contains essays on specific classroom practices, particularly in technical and business writing.

144. *College English*. Urbana, IL: National Council of Teachers of English, Monthly. (205-348-6488)

Concentrates on articles written by and for teachers of English at the college level. Formerly entitled *English Journal*, theoretical discussions and articles with professional advice are offered.

145. *Communication Briefings*. Blackwood, NJ: Encoders, Inc., Monthly. (609-589-3503)

Intended for public relations and communications executives, the journal examines ideas and techniques in public relations, media relations, speeches and employee/manager relations. Interviews with communicators and experts, book reviews, and abstracts of articles from other journals are included.

146. *Communication Illustrated*. Bartlesville, OK: Joe Williams Communications, Monthly. (918-336-2267)

The newsletter is designed to improve employee communications through information on programs, conferences and publications for communicators.

147. *Communication Monographs*. Annandale, VA: Speech Communication Association, Quarterly. (703-750-0533)

The research articles and brief reports published deal with human communication processes. Areas such as interpersonal communication, small group interaction and public address are studied.

148. *Communication News*. Washington, DC: American Society of Association Executives, Monthly. (202-626-2723)

Written for professional association communicators, the newsletter gives advice on the writing, editing and improvement of publications. There are additional comments on conventions, courses, jobs and relevant legal and legislative actions.

149. *Communication World*. San Francisco, CA: International Association of Business Communicators, Monthly. (415-433-3400)

Formerly called *IABC News* and the *IABC Journal*, the journal has interviews, news and articles in organizational communications. Book reviews, a buyers guide, consultants directory and other useful features are displayed for communications and public relations professionals.

150. *Decker Communications Report*. Madison, WI: Magna Publications, Monthly. (608-249-2455)

This is a newsletter for business executives. Techniques are revealed for improving speaking and presentation skills.

151. *EWN: Editor's Workshop Newsletter*. Chicago, IL: Lawrence Ragan Communications, Monthly. (312-922-8245)

Advice is furnished for writing, editing and speechwriting in organizational communications. The newsletter, for professionals, features a technology and equipment update and a calendar of events.

152. *IEEE Transactions on Professional Communication*. New York: Institute of Electrical and Electronics Engineers, Quarterly. (212-750-7900)

Formerly entitled *IEEE Transactions on Engineering Writing and Speech*, the journal is concerned with the study, development and improvement of writing and editing in the electrical and electronics fields. Research, practical advice and book reviews are reported for those involved in improving professional communications.

153. *Intercom.* Washington, DC: Society for Technical Communication, Ten times per year. (202-737-0035)

Communications topics discussed are writing, editing and publications management. Intended for writers, editors, educators and engineers, the journal presents new developments in technical communication. Those interested in the theory and practice of technical communication can review news of the association its members.

154. *Issues in Writing.* Stevens Point, WI: Department of English, University of Wisconsin - Stevens Point, Semi-annual.

This refereed journal began in fall 1988. It is devoted to the study of writing in science, business, the professions and related areas. Aimed at both academics and professionals, the publications supports teachers and publishes the writing of practitioners.

155. *Journal of Advanced Composition.* Mobile, AL: Department of English, University of South Alabama, Semi-annual. (205-460-6146).

The teaching of advanced writing in college is studied. The journal considers both the theory and practice of business, technical and professional writing.

156. *Journal of Business Communication.* Urbana, IL: University of Illinois, Quarterly. (217-333-1007)

Formerly the *ABCA Journal of Business Communication*, this journal is published by the Association for Business Communication. It emphasizes research articles on the theory and techniques of business communication. Both corporate and classroom situations are covered.

157. *Journal of Communication.* Fair Lawn, NJ: Oxford University Press, Quarterly. (212-679-7300)

Concerned with the study of communication, this publication focuses on the study of communication in human relations. Articles study theory, practice and policy. The articles, brief reports, book reviews and news notes are devoted to significant problems and issues in communications.

158. *Journal of Technical Writing and Communication.* Farmingdale, NY: Baywood Publishing Company, Quarterly. (516-249-2464)

A major professional and scholarly journal for practitioners and teachers, articles are published on the theory and practice of professional writing. Technical journalism, business communication, intercultural communication, and other areas are among those studied. The journal provides pieces on techniques and research and tend to stress theory.

159. *Make It Happen.* Portland, OR: Action Marketing, Monthly. (503-287-8321)

The newsletter has how-to articles and suggestions in business communication and marketing. Aimed at the Portland metropolitan area, it investigates networking, computer systems and other topics of interest to professionals.

160. *Management Communication Quarterly.* Newberry Park, CA: Sage Publications, Quarterly. (805-499-0721)

This new journal contains material on writing, presentations and interpersonal communication. Recent issues have covered conflict styles in organiations, collaborative writing and annual reports. Book reviews, guest commentaries, research notes and measuring instruments are featured.

161. *Newsletter on Newsletters.* Rhinebeck, NY: Newsletter Clearinghouse, Semi-monthly. (914-876-2081)

Information on the management, editing and promotion of newsletters is related in a publication for newsletter professionals.

162. *The Ragan Report.* Chicago, IL: Lawrence Ragan Communications, Weekly. (312-922-8245)

For public relations practitioners and organizational communicators, techniques are advanced on writing, photography and design. Communications executives will find how-to advice, editorials, book reviews, and a calendar of events.

163. *Simply Stated.* Washington, DC: American Institutes for Research, Document Design Center, Ten times per year. (202-342-5000)

Advice is given on technical writing and editing. There are practical articles, editorials, book reviews, conference reports and recommended reading.

164. *Speechwriter's Newsletter.* Chicago, IL: Lawrence Ragan Communications, Weekly. (312-922-8245)

This is a newsletter for corporate and political speechwriters. Speech writing tips, examples and criticism is revealed.

165. *Teaching English in the Two-Year College.* Urbana, IL: National Council of Teachers of Education, Quarterly. (919-757-6383)

The articles published should be of interest to teachers in two-year college systems. Business and technical writing are two of the topics discussed.

166. *Technical Communication.* Washington, DC: Society for Technical Communication, Quarterly. (202-737-0035)

The journal has articles of professional interest to technical communicators. Practical articles for technical writers and editors are stressed. Most of the articles are written by working professionals and feature problem-solving approaches to writing, editing, production, management and teaching.

167. *The Technical Writing Teacher.* St. Paul, MN: Association of Teachers of Technical Writing, Three times per year. (806-742-2517)

The contents support technical writing for teachers. There are exercises, assignments and programs for classroom use. Book reviews are also included.

168. *Training and Development Journal.* Alexandria, VA: American Society for Training and Development, Monthly. (703-683-8100)

Formerly called *Training Directors Journal,* this publication reflects the interests of management and personnel practitioners. As considerable emphasis is placed on good communication, the reports examine to business, technical and organizational communication.

Chapter 3

INFORMATION SOURCES

Questions sometimes require immediate answers when either no published source exists or there is no time to locate one. This chapter is a guide to solving information problems with data obtained from alternate sources such as national associations, government agencies, grammar hotlines, book publishers and research institutions. In supplementing print and database sources, these services and agencies can help improve the quality of written and oral communication products.

The writing process demands a knowledge of grammar and punctuation rules that many of us have lost through disuse. Grammar hotlines, usually associated with colleges or universities, have sprung up in response to this need. Hotline staffs will answer punctuation, grammar and usage needs over the telephone. Several U. S. agencies publish important journals and reports related to business and technical communication. The agencies also serve the community by replying to telephone queries.

National associations and research institutions sponsor publications (newsletters and journals) and meetings (conferences and seminars). They promote networking and the exchange of ideas between industry professionals. This information can be tapped through memberships, subscriptions, and telephone referrals. While regional libraries are always one valuable resource for such materials, copies of important books can be ordered directly from their publishers.

ASSOCIATIONS

169. ACCE Communications Council. c/o Rosemary M. Harper, 4232 King St., Alexandria, VA 22203. (703-998-0072)

This association of editors, advertising managers, business managers, and creative personnel sponsors seminars and an advisory service. Associated with the Chambers of Commerce , the Council assists in the development and improvement of communications programs and speakers bureaus.

170. Academy of Management. P.O. Drawer KZ, Mississippi State University, Mississippi State, MS 39762. (601-325-7014)

The association, for management professors and executives, publishes two quarterly journals and a newsletter. One of the publications, the *Journal of the*

Academy of Management, often has articles dealing with organizational communications.

171. American Society for Information Science. 1424 16th St., N.W., Suite 404, Washington, DC 20036. (202-462-1000)

Those interested in the use, organization, storage, retrieval, evaluation and dissemination of information formed this society. Improvement of the information transfer process through education and the application of research is promoted. The Society issues several journals in the area of information science, including *ASIS Journal.*

172. American Society for Training and Development. Box 1443, 1630 Duke St., Alexandria, VA 22313. (703-683-8100)

This society is composed of individuals involved in training and development. It serves an educational function, with annual seminars, and a monthly journal, *Training and Development Journal.*

173. American Society of Business Press Editors. 4445 Gilmer Ln., Cleveland, OH 44143. (216-531-8306)

For editors of business and technical publications, the society researches editorial problems and practices. It acts as a forum for the exchange of ideas between members.

174. Associated Business Writers of America. 1450 S. Havana, Suite 620, Aurora, CO 80012. (303-751-7844)

The association seeks to establish communication between editors and freelance writers. Through it business editors locate writers specializing in business writing.

175. Association for Business Communication. 100 English Building, 608 S. Wright St., University of Illinois, Urbana, IL 61801. (217-333-1007)

This is the core association for those in business and technical writing. Developed from the American Business Writers Association, it arranges research programs and publishes both a bulletin and the *Journal of Business Communication.*

176. Association for Education in Journalism and Mass Communication. College of Journalism, 1621 College St., University of South Carolina, Columbia, SC 29208. (803-777-2005)

The professional organization of college and university journalism teachers, it seeks to improve teaching methods and stimulate research. The association compiles statistics and puts out three journals and a newsletter, among them *Journalism Educator* and *Journalism Monographs.*

177. Association of Teachers of Technical Writing. c/o Dr. Carolyn D. Rude, Department of English, Box 4530, Texas Tech University, Lubbock, TX 79409. (806-742-2517)

Its primary purpose is to promote communication among teachers. The teachers are given bibliographies of teaching materials and informed of current research. The association issues a journal, *Technical Writing Teacher*.

178. Conference on College Composition and Communication. 111 Kenyon Rd., Urbana, IL 61801. (217-328-3870)

While primaily an organization of college and university teachers of English, the group has relevance for teachers of technical and business writing. Among its publications is *College Composition and Communication*.

179. Council of Communication Management. Box 3970, Grand Central Post Office, New York, NY 10163. (212-254-3985)

This is an organization of company individuals responsible for communication with the public, the government and company employees.

180. Institute of Electrical and Electronics Engineers, Professional Communications Society. 345 E. 47th St., New York, NY 10017. (212-705-7900)

Part of the I.E.E.E., the Professional Communications section is composed of technical writers, editors, publication managers, teachers and engineers. It studies, develops and promotes techniques for the preparation, organization and dissemination of information in electronics. Members receive the quarterly journal, *IEEE Transaction on Professional Communication*.

181. International Association for Mass Communication Research. Centre for Mass Communication Research, University of Leicester, 104 Regent Road, Leicester LE1 7LT England, UK. (533-523864)

Sections of the association are concerned with communications technology, international communication and professional education. It publishes monographs and reports of sponsored symposia.

182. International Association of Business Communicators. 870 Market St., Suite 940, San Francisco, CA 94102. (415-433-3400)

Composed primarily of business and industry professionals, organizational communication is researched, establishment of college-level curricula encouraged, and the exchange of ideas fostered. *Communication World* and an annual directory form part of the I.A.B.C.'s offerings.

183. International Communications Association. P.O. Box 9589, Austin, TX 78766. (512-454-8299)

The group's divisions specialize in interpersonal and organizational communication. Systematic study is encouraged and research results are applied to communication practices and skills. For those interested in studying the nature of human communication, two journals (*Human Communication Research, Journal of Communication*), a newsletter, a yearbook and an annual volume of abstracts are published.

184. International Council for Technical Communication. c/o E. N. White, 477 Reading Road, Winnersh, Wokingham, Berkshire RG11 5HX, England, UK. (734-781339)

Nine countries have joined together to establish standards and codes of practice on the communication of technical and related information.

185. International Society for General Semantics. P.O. Box 2469, San Francisco, CA 94126. (415-543-1747)

The society inquires into general semantics through publications, lectures and research. Members are educators and professionals interested in improving communication.

186. National Council of Teachers of English. 1111 Kenyon Rd., Urbana, IL 61801. (217-328-3870)

Teachers of English, at all levels, have joined together to improve teaching effectiveness. Several important journals published by N.C.T.E. have articles on business and technical writing, including *College English* and *College Composition and Communication*.

187. Society for Technical Communication. 815 Fifteenth Street N.W., Washington, DC 20005. (202-737-0035)

Formed through the merger of several organizations and incorporated in 1958, this group consists of writers, editors and teachers of technical publications. Its purpose is the advancement of technical communication theory and practice, the encouragement of research, and the development of training programs. The journal, *Technical Communication*, is issued to members.

188. Society of Publication Designers. 60 E. 42nd St., Suite 1130, New York, NY 10165. (212-983-8585)

The association is for those responsible for the layout and design of consumer, business and professional publications and newspapers. The society sponsors a newsletter and holds an annual design competition.

GOVERNMENT AGENCY TELEPHONE NUMBERS

The agencies of the U.S. government prepare a variety of reports and other documents. These can be located with the indexes and databases described in Chapter 2. Information about the departments, their activities and personnel can be found through the directories listed in Chapter 1. The agencies will answer telephone queries about publications and other informational needs. For that purpose, the telephone numbers (800 numbers where possible) of important agencies and departments are given here.

189. Bureau of the Census. 301-763-4040

International Trade Administration 202-377-3808
Minority Business Development Agency 202-377-1936

190. Department of Commerce.

Business Liaison 202-377-3942
General Number 202-377-2000
Information 202-377-1200
Publications 202-377-2495, 800-424-5197

191. Department of Education.

General Number 202-245-3192
Information 202-732-4576
Information Center 202-245-3192
Publications 800-424-1616

192. Department of Labor.

General Number 202-523-8165
Information 202-523-7316
Publications (Bureau of Labor Statistics) 202-523-1221

193. National Bureau of Standards.

General Number 301-975-2000
Information 301-975-3058
Publications 301-975-3058

194. National Technical Information Service.

Information 202-377-3263
Publications 703-487-4650

195. Securities Exchange Commission.

General Number 202-272-3100
Information (SEC Reading Room) 202-272-7450
Consumer activities 202-272-7440
Office of Public Affairs 202-272-2650

196. Small Business Administration.

Information (Answer Desk) 202-653-7561,800-368-5855
Publications 202-653-6668

GRAMMAR HOTLINES

The grammar hotlines offer answers to short questions about writing, grammar, punctuation, spelling, diction and syntax. Most of the services are staffed by graduate students, faculty or retired teachers. Because they are associated with colleges and universities, most reduce or suspend service between semesters and during the summer. The hotlines, unless otherwise noted, do not accept collect calls and will return long-distance calls collect. The information contained in the 1989 *Grammar Hotline Directory* is reprinted here with the permission of the Writing Center/Grammar Hotline, Tidewater Community College, Virginia Beach, Virginia.

Alabama

197. Writing Center Hotline, Auburn University, Auburn, AL 36849.

205-826-5749   Peter Huggins

Open Monday-Thursday, 9:00 am to noon and 1:00 pm to 4:00 pm; Friday 9:00 am to noon; reduced hours in summer.

198. Grammar Hotline, Jacksonville State University, Jacksonville, AL 36265.
205-231-5409   Carol Cauthen, Dr. Clyde Cox

Open Monday-Friday, 8:00 am to 4:30 pm.

199. Grammar Hotline, University of Alabama, Tuscaloosa, AL 35487.
205-348-5049   Carol Howell

Open Monday-Thursday, 8:30 am to 4:00 pm; Tuesday-Wednesday, 6:00 pm to 8:00 pm; Friday, 9:00 am to 1:00 pm; summer hours, 8:30 am to 1:00 pm.

Arizona

200. Grammar Hotline, Arizona State University, Tempe, AZ 85287.
602-967-0378   Dr. J. J. Lamberts

Monday-Friday, 8:00 am to 5:00 pm.

Arkansas

201. The Writers Hotline, University of Arkansas, Little Rock, AR 72204.
501-569-3162   Marilynn Keys

Open Monday-Friday, 8:00 am to noon.

California

202. National Grammar Hotline, Moorpark College, Moorpark, CA 93021.
805-529-2321   Michael Strumpf

Open Monday-Friday, 8:00 am to noon, September-June.

203. English Helpline, Cosumnes River College, Sacramento, CA 95823.
916-686-7444   Billie Miller Cooper

Monday-Friday, 9:00 am to 11:45 am, fall and spring semesters; 24-hour recorder.

Colorado

204. USC Grammar Hotline, University of Southern Colorado, Pueblo, CO 81001.
303-549-2787   Margaret Senatore, Ralph Dille

Open Monday-Friday, 9:30 am to 3:30 pm; reduced hours from May 15 - August 25.

Delaware

205. Grammar Hotline, University of Delaware, Newark, DE 19716.
302-451-1890   Margaret P. Hassert

Open Monday-Thursday, 9:00 am to noon, 1:00 pm to 5:00 pm, and 6:00 pm to 9:00 pm; Friday, 9:00 am to noon and 1:00 pm to 5:00 pm.

Florida

206. Writing Lab and Grammar Hotline, University of West Florida, Pensacola, FL 32514.

904-474-2129   Mamie Webb Hixon

Open Monday-Thursday, 9:00 am to 5:00 pm; occasional evening hours; Friday and summer hours vary.

Georgia

207. Writing Center, Georgia State University, Atlanta, GA 30303.

404-651-2906   Patricia Graves

Open Monday-Thursday, 8:30 am to 5:00 pm; Friday, 8:30 am to 3:00 pm; evening hours vary.

Illinois

208. Grammar Hotline, Eastern Illinois University, Charleston, IL 61920.

217-581-5929   Jeanne Simpson

Open Monday-Friday, 10:00 am to 3:00 pm; summer hours vary.

209. The Write Line, Oakton Community College, Des Plaines, IL 60016.

312-635-1948   Richard Francis Tracz

Open September-May, 10:00 am to 2:00 pm; summer hours vary.

210. Grammar Hotline, Illinois State University, Normal, IL 61761.

309-438-2345   Janice Neuleib, Maurice Scharton

Open Monday-Friday, 8:00 am to 4:30 pm.

211. Grammarline, Illinois Valley Community College, Oglesby, IL 61348.

815-224-2720   Robert Howard, Robert Mueller

Open Monday-Friday, 8:00 am to 4:00 pm.

212. Grammarphone, Triton College, River Grove, IL 60171.

312-456-0300, ext. 254   Hillard Hebda

Open Monday-Thursday, 8:30 am to 9:00 pm; Friday, 8:30 am to 4:00 pm; Saturday, 10:00 am to 1:00 pm.

Indiana

213. IUPUI Writing Hotline, Indiana University-Purdue University at Indianapolis, University Writing Center, Indianapolis, IN 46202.

317-274-3000   Barbara Cambridge

Open Monday-Thursday, 9:00 am to 4:00 pm.

214. Grammar Crisis Line, The Writing Center, Ball State University, Muncie, IN 47306.

317-285-8387   Paul W. Ranieri

Open Monday-Thursday, 9:00 am to 8:00 pm; Friday, 9:00 am to 5:00 pm, September-May; Monday-Friday, 11:00 am to 2:00 pm, May-August.

215. Grammar Hotline, Purdue University, West Lafayette, IN 47907.

317-494-3723   Muriel Harris

Open Monday-Friday, 9:30 am to 4:00 pm, when a writing instructor is available during spring, summer, and fall semesters; closed between semesters.

Kansas

216. Writer's Hotline, Emporia State University, Emporia, KS 66801.

316-343-5380   Robert Goltra

Open Monday-Thursday, noon to 5:00 pm; Wednesday, 7:00 pm to 9:00 pm; summer hours vary.

Louisiana

217. Grammar Hotline, University of Southwestern Louisiana, Lafayette, LA 70504.

318-231-5224   James McDonald

Open Monday-Thursday, 8:00 am to 4:00 pm; Friday, 8:00 am to 3:00 pm

Maryland

218. Writers Hotline, University of Maryland Baltimore County, Baltimore, MD 21228.

301-455-2585   Barbara Cooper, Department of English

Open Monday-Friday, 10:00 am to noon, September-May.

219. Grammarphone (patented trademark), Frostburg State University, Frostburg, MD 21532.

301-689-4327   Glynn Baugher, Department of English

Open Monday-Friday, 10:00 am to noon.

Massachusetts

220. Grammar Hotline, North Shore Community College, Lynn, MA 01901.

617-593-7284   Marilyn Dorfman

Open Monday-Friday, 8:30 am to 4:00 pm.

221. Grammar Hotline, Northeastern University, Boston, MA 02115.
617-437-2512   Stuart Peterfreund, English Department

Open Monday-Friday, 8:30 am to 4:30 pm; summer hours vary.

Michigan

222. Grammar Hotline, C.S. Mott Community College, Flint, MI 48503.
313-762-0229   Leatha Terwilliger

Open Monday-Thursday, 8:30 am to 3:30 pm; Friday, 8:30 am to 12:30 pm;
Tuesday-Wednesday, 5:30 pm to 8:30 pm; summer hours vary.

223. Writer's Hotline, Western Michigan University, Kalamazoo, MI 49008.
616-387-4442   Eileen B. Evans

Open Monday-Friday, 9:00 am to 4:00 pm; summer hours vary.

224. Writer's Hotline, Lansing Community College, Lansing, MI 48901.
517-483-1040   Dr. George R. Bramer

Open Monday-Friday, 9:00 am to 4:00 pm.

Missouri

225. Grammar Hotline, Missouri Southern State College, Joplin, MS 64801.
417-624-0171   Dale W. Simpson

Open Monday-Friday, 8:30 am to 4:30 pm.

226. Writer's Hotline, University of Missouri - Kansas City, Kansas City, MS
64110.
816-276-2244   Judy McCormick, David Foster, Karen Doerr

Open Monday-Friday, 9:00 am to 4:00 pm

New Jersey

227. Grammar Hotline, Jersey City State College, Jersey City, NJ 07305.
201-547-3337, 201-547-3338   Harlan Hamilton

Open Monday-Friday, 9:00 am to 4:30 pm; summer Monday-Thursday, 8:00 am
to 5:00 pm

New York

228. Rewrite, York College, City University of New York, Jamaica, NY 11451.
718-739-7483   Joan Baum, Alan Cooper

Open Monday-Friday, 1:00 pm to 4:00 pm.

North Carolina

229. Grammar Hotline, Methodist College, Fayetteville, NC 28301.
919-488-7110   Robert Christian, Sue L. Kimball, James X. Ward

Open Monday-Friday, 8:00 am to 5:00 pm.

230. Grammar Hotline, East Carolina University, Greenville, NC 27858.
919-757-6728, 919-757-6399   Dr. Jo Allen

Open Monday-Thursday, 8:00 am to 4:00 pm; Friday, 8:00 am to 3:00 pm; Tuesday and Thursday 6:00 pm to 9:00 pm.

Ohio

231. Dial-A-Grammar, Raymond Walters College, Cincinnati, OH 45236.
513-745-5731   Dr. Phyllis A. Sherwood

Tapes requests, returns calls. Long distance calls are returned collect.

232. Writer's Remedies, University of Cincinnati, Cincinnati, OH 45221.
513-475-2493   Jay A. Yarmove

Open Monday-Friday, 9:00 am to 10:00 am; 1:00 pm to 2:00 pm.

233. Writing Center Hotline, Cincinnati Technical College, Cincinnati, OH 45223.
513-569-1736, 513-569-1737   John Battistone, Catherine Rahmes

Open Monday-Thursday, 8:00 am to 8:00 pm; Friday, 8:00 am to 4:00 pm; Saturday, 9:00 am to 1:00 pm.

234. Grammar Hotline, Cuyahoga Community College, Cleveland, OH 44122.
216-987-2050   Margaret Taylor

Open Monday-Friday, 1:00 pm to 3:00 pm; Sunday-Thursday, 7:00 pm to 10:00 pm; twenty-four hour answering machine.

235. Writer's Hotline, Wright State University, Dayton, OH 45435.
513-873-2158   Maura Taaffe

Open Monday-Friday, 9:00 am to 4:00 pm.

236. Writing Resource Center, Ohio Wesleyan University, Delaware, OH 43015.
614-369-4431, ext. 301   Dr. Ulle Lewes, Jean Hopper

Open Monday-Friday, 9:00 am to noon, 1:00 pm to 4:00pm; September-May.

Oklahoma

237. Grammar Hotline, Southern Nazarene University, Bethany, OK 73008.

405-491-6328; June - August call 405-354-1739   Jim Wilcox, Department of English

Open Monday-Friday, 9:00 am to 4:00 pm.

238. Grammar Service, Chickasha, OK 73018.

405-224-8622   Virginia Lee Underwood, retired teacher and editor

Open Monday-Friday, 9:00 am to 5:00 pm; Saturday, 9:00 am to noon. Service offered through her home; long distance calls returned collect.

Pennsylvania

239. Academic Support Center, Cedar Crest College, Allentown, PA 18104.

215-437-4471   Karen Coleman, Priscilla Johnson

Open Monday-Friday, 10:00 am to 3:00 pm; September - May.

240. Burger Associates, Glen Mills, PA 19342.

215-399-1130   Robert S. Burger, former teacher

Open Monday-Friday, 8:00 am to 5:00 pm.

241. Grammar Hotline, Lincoln University, Lincoln University, PA 19352.

215-932-8300, ext. 460   Carolyn L. Simpson

Open Monday-Friday, 9:00 am to 5:00 pm; summer hours vary.

242. Grammar Hotline, Coalition for Adult Literacy, Pittsburgh, PA 15104.

412-344-9759   Dr. Mary Newton Bruder

Open Monday, Wednesday, Friday, 9:00 am to 5:00 pm, September-mid June; recorder takes messages at other times.

South Carolina

243. Writer's Hotline, The Citadel Writing Center, Charleston, SC 29409.

803-792-3194   Angela W. Williams

Open Monday-Friday, 8:00 am to 4:00 pm; Sunday-Thursday, 6:00 pm to 10:00 pm.

244. Writer's Hotline, University of South Carolina, Columbia, SC 29208.

803-777-7020   Laurie Demarest, Suzanne Moore

Open Monday-Friday, 8:30 am to 5:00 pm.

245. Grammar Hotline, Converse College, Spartanburg, SC 29301.

803-596-9613   Dr. Karen Carmean, Eva Pratt

Open Tuesday-Thursday, noon to 5:00 pm.

Texas

246. Grammarphone, Amarillo College, Amarillo, TX 79178.

806-374-4726   Patricia Maddox, Carl Fowler

Open Monday-Thursday, 8:00 am to 9:00 pm; Friday, 8:00 am to 3:00 pm; Sunday, 2:00 pm to 6:00 pm.

247. Downtown Grammar Line, University of Houston Downtown, Houston, TX 77002.

713-221-8670   Linda Coblentz

Open Monday-Thursday, 9:00 am to 4:00 pm; Friday, 9:00 am to 1:00 pm; summer hours, Monday-Thursday, 10:30 am to 4:00 pm.

248. Learning Line, San Antonio College, San Antonio, TX 78284.

512-733-2503   Leon Ricketts, Irma Luna

Open Monday-Thursday, 8:00 am to 9:00 pm; Friday 8:00 am to 4:00 pm.

Virginia

249. Writing Helpline, Northern Virginia Community College, Sterling, VA 22170.

703-450-2511   Diane M. Rhodes, London Campus

Open Monday-Thursday, 10:00 am to 2:00 pm.

250. Grammar Hotline, Tidewater Community College, Virginia Beach, VA 23456.

804-427-7170   Donna Reiss, Writing Center

Open Monday-Friday, 10:00 am to noon; afternoon hours vary; reduced hours in summer.

Wisconsin

251. Grammar Hotline, Northeast Wisconsin Technical Institute, Green Bay, WI 54307.

414-498-5427   Rose Marie Mastricola, Joanne Rathburn

Open Monday-Thursday, 8:30 am to 8:00 pm; Friday, 8:00 am to 4:00 pm.

252. Grammar Hotline, University of Wisconsin, Platteville, WI 53818.

608-342-1615   Nancy Daniels

Open Monday-Thursday, 9:00 am to 4:00 pm; Friday, 9:00 am to noon.

Canada

253. Grammar Hotline, Grant MacEwan Community College, Edmonton, Alberta, Canada.

403-441-4699   Lois Drew

Open Tuesday-Friday, 12:30 pm to 3:30 pm.

254. Grammar Hotline, University of New Brunswick, Fredericton, New Brunswick, Canada.

506-459-3631 (residence)   A. M. Kinloch

Variable hours.

PUBLISHERS OF BUSINESS AND TECHNICAL COMMUNICATION BOOKS

255. Acropolis Books, 2400 Seventeenth St., N.W., Washington, DC 20009. (202-387-6805, 800-451-7771, 800-621-5199 in DC)

256. Addison-Wesley, 1 Jacob Way, Reading MA 01867.   (617-944-3700, 800-447-2226)

257. Alfred Publishing Company, 16380 Roscoe Blvd., No. 200, Van Nuys, CA 91406. (800-292-6122)

258. Allen and Unwin, 8 Winchester Pl., Winchester, MA 01890. (818-891-5999, 800-292-6122, 800-821-6083 in CA)

259. Allyn and Bacon, 160 Gould St., Needham Heights, MA 02194. (617-455-1200, 800-852-8024, 800-223-1360 orders)

260. AMACOM, 135 W. Fiftieth St., New York, NY 10020. (212-903-8315)

261. American Business Communication Association, Association for Business Communication,100   English Bldg., 608 S. Wright St., University of Illinois, Urbana, IL 61801. (217-333-1007)

262. American Institutes for Research, P.O. Box 1113, Palo Alto, CA 94302. (415-493-3550)

263. American Society for Metals, ASM International, Metals Park, OH 44073. (216-338-5151)

264. American Society of Association Executives, 1575 Eye St. N.W., Washington, DC 20005. (202-626-2723)

265. Arco Publishing, 1 Gulf and Western Bldg., New York, NY 10023. (212-373-8931, 201-767-5054 orders)

266. Asher-Gallant Press, 201 Montrose Rd., Westbury, NY 11590. (516-333-7440)

267. Bantam Books, 666 Fifth Ave., New York, NY 10103. (800-223-6834)

268. Barron's Educational Series, P.O. Box 8040, 250 Wireless Blvd., Hauppauge, NY 11788 (800-645-3476, 800-257-5729 in NY)

269. Beaufort Books, 9 E. Fortieth St., New York, NY 10016. (212-685-2928, 800-526-7626)

270. Bingley, Clive, 7 Ridgmount St., London WC1E 7AE UK. (01-636-7543)

271. Bobbs-Merrill, 866 Third Ave., New York, NY 10022. (212-702-2000, 800-257-5755)

272. Bowker, R. R., 245 W. Seventeenth St., New York, NY 10011. (800-521-8110, 800-431-1713, 800-537-8416 in Canada)

273. Brown, William C., 2460 Kerper Blvd., Dubuque, IA 52001. (319-588-1451, 800-338-5578 orders)

274. Bureau of National Affairs, 1231 Twenty-fifth St. N.W., Washington, DC 20037. (202-452-4200)

275. Business Books, Box 6870-51, Torrance, CA 90504. (213-831-2770)

276. Chilton Book Company, Chilton Way, Radnor, PA 19089. (800-345-1214)

277. Conference Board, The, 845 Third Ave., New York, NY 10022. (212-759-0900, 800-872-6273)

278. Contemporary Books, 180 N. Michigan Ave., Chicago, IL 60601. (312-782-9181)

279. Curtin and London, P.O. Box 363, Marblehead, MA 01945. (617-631-0762)

280. Dame Publications, 7800 Bissonnet, Suite 415, Houston, TX 77074. (713-995-1000)

281. Dell Publishing Company, 1 Dag Hammarskjold Plaza, 245 E. Forty-seventh St., New York,NY 10017. (212-765-6500, 800-255-4133)

282. Delmar Publishers, 2 Computer Dr. W., Albany, NY 12205. (800-347-7707, 800-252-2550 in NY)

283. Dembner Books, 80 Eighth Ave., New York, NY 10011. (212-924-2525, 800-223-2584)

284. Digital Press, 12 Crosby Dr., BUO/E94, Bedford, MA 01730. (617-276-1536, 800-343-8321)

285. Dodd, Mead and Company, 71 Fifth Ave., New York, NY 10003. (212-627-8444, 800-237-3255, 800-544-4463 in NY)

286. Dow Jones-Irwin, 1818 Ridge Rd., Homewood, IL 60430. (312-798-6000, 800-323-4560)

287. Dryden Press, 901 N. Elm, Hinsdale, IL 60521. (312-325-2985, 800-323-7437)

288. Facts on File, 460 Park Ave. S., New York, NY 10016. (212-683-2244, 800-322-8755)

289. Fell, Frederick, Publishers, 2131 Hollywood Blvd., Suite 204, Hollywood, FL 33020. (305-925-5242, 800-526-7626)

290. Free Press, 866 Third Ave., New York, NY 10022. (212-702-2004, 800-257-5755)

291. Gorsuch Scarisbrick Publishers, 8233 Via Paseo del Norte, Suite E400, Scottsdale, AZ 85258. (602-991-7881)

292. Gower Publishing Company, Old Post Road, Brookfield, VT 05036. (802-276-3162)

293. Greenwood Press, 88 Post Road W., Box 5007, Westport, CT 06881. (203-226-3571)

294. Gulf Publishing Company, P.O. Box 2608, Houston, TX 77252. (713-529-4301)

295. Harcourt Brace Jovanovich, 1250 Sixth Ave., San Diego, CA 92101. (619-699-6335, 800-543-1918)

296. Harper and Row, 10 E. Fifty-third St., New York, NY 10022. (212-207-7000, 800-242-7737, 800-982-4377 in PA)

297. Heath, D. C., 125 Spring St., Lexington, MA 02173. (800-334-3284)

298. Hilger, Adam, Techno House, Redcliffe Way, Bristol, England BS1 6NX, UK. (Bristol 276693)

299. Holt, Rinehart and Winston, 111 Fifth Ave., New York, NY 10003. (212-614-3300, 800-782-4479)

300. Houghton Mifflin, 1 Beacon St., Boston, MA 02108. (617-725-5000, 800-225-3362)

301.   ICSA Publishing (Woodhead-Faulkner), Fitzwilliam House, 32 Trumpington St., Cambridge, England CB2 1QY, UK. (Cambridge 66733)

302. ISI Press, 3501 Market St., Philadelphia, PA 19104. (215-386-0100, 800-523-1850)

303. Institute of Electrical and Electronics Engineers, 345 E. Forty-seventh St., New York, NY 10017. (212-705-7900)

304. Institute of Financial Education, 111 E. Wacker Dr., Chicago, Il 60601. (312-644-3100)

305. Irwin, Richard D., 1818 Ridge Rd., Homewood, IL 60430. (312-798-6000, 800-323-4560 (faculty), 800-634-3961 orders)

306. **Kendall/Hunt Publishing,** 2460 Kerper Blvd., Dubuque, IA 52001. (319-588-1451)

307. **Kent Publications,** 18301 Halstead St., Northridge, CA 91325. (818-349-2080)

308. **Lebhar-Friedman Books,** 425 Park Ave., New York, NY 10022. (212-371-9400)

309. **Lewis Publishers,** 121 S. Main St., P.O. Drawer 519, Chelsea, MI 48118. (313-475-8619, 800-525-7894)

310. **Little, Brown and Company,** 34 Beacon St., Boston, MA 02108. (617-227-0730, 800-343-9204)

311. **Longman Financial Services Institute,** 520 N. Dearborn St., Chicago, IL 60610. (312-836-0466, 800-428-3852, 800-428-3846 orders)

312. **Macdonald and Evans,** 128 Long Acre, London, England WC2E 9AN, UK. (01-379-7383)

313. **McGraw-Hill,** 1221 Ave of the Americas, New York, NY 10020. (212-512-2000, 800-262-4729 retail, 800-722-4726 consumer)

314. **Macmillan,** 866 Third Ave., New York, NY 10022. (212-702-2000, 800-257-5755)

315. **McQuaid, Robert W.,** 4853 Mt. Elbrus Dr., San Diego, CA 92117. (619-279-5827)

316. **Merrill Publishing Company,** 1300 Alum Creek Dr., Columbus, OH 43216. (614-258-8441, 800-848-1567, 800-848-6205 orders)

317. **Morrow, William,** 105 Madison Ave., New York, NY 10016. (212-889-3050, 800-843-9389)

318. **National Publishers,** P.O. Box 8042, Van Nuys, CA 91409. (818-705-8865)

319. **National Textbook Company,** 4255 W. Touhy Ave., Lincolnwood, IL 60646. (312-679-5500, 800-323-4900)

320. **New American Library,** 1633 Broadway, New York, NY 10019. (212-397-8000, 800-526-0275 orders)

321. **New York Institute of Finance,** 70 Pine St., New York, NY 10270. (212-344-2900)

322. **NFER-Nelson Publishing Company,** Darville House, 2 Oxford Road E., Windsor, Berkshire SL4 1DF, UK. (Windsor 858961)

323. **Nichols Publishing Company,** P.O. Box 96, New York, NY 10024. (212-580-8079)

324. **Nolo Press,** 950 Parker St., Berkeley, CA 94710. (415-549-1976, 800-445-6656)

325. **Osborne McGraw-Hill,** 2600 Tenth St., Berkeley, CA 94710. (415-548-2805, 800-227-0900)

326. **PSI Research,** 720 S. Hillview Dr., Milpitas, CA 95035. (408-263-9671, 800-228-2275, 800-221-4089 in CA)

327. **Pergamon Press,** Maxwell House, Fairview Pk., Elmsford, NY 10523. (914-592-7700)

328. **Petrocelli Books,** Research Park, 251 Wall St., Princeton, NJ 08540. (609-924-5851)

329. **Pilot Books,** 103 Cooper St., Babylon, NY 11702. (516-422-2225)

330. **Prentice-Hall,** Rte. 9W, Englewood Cliffs, NJ 07632. (201-592-2000, 800-634-2863)

331. **Prima Publishing and Communications,** P.O. Box 1260, Rocklin, CA 95677. (916-624-5718)

332. **Ragan, Lawrence, Communications,** 407 S. Dearborn St., Chicago, IL 60605. (312-922-8245)

333. **Rand McNally and Company,** P.O. Box 7600, Chicago, IL 60680. (312-673-9100, 800-323-4070)

334. **Random House,** 201 E. Fiftieth St., New York, NY 10022. (212-751-2600, 800-638-6460)

335. **Research Enterprises Publications,** 4701 Kenmore Ave., Suite 905, Alexandria, VA 22304. (703-370-4044)

336. **Research Press,** 2612 N. Mattis Ave., Champaign, IL 61821. (217-352-3273)

337. **Richardson and Steirman,** 246 Fifth Ave., New York, NY 10001. (212-213-1203, 800-526-7626)

338. **Routledge, Chapman and Hall,** 29 W. Thirty-fifth St., New York, NY 10001. (212-224-3336)

339. **Royall Press,** P.O. Box 9022, San Rafael, CA 94912. (415-885-1484)

340. **St. Martin's Press,** 175 Fifth Ave., New York, NY 10010. (212-674-5151, 800-221-7945)

341. **Scarecrow Press,** 52 Liberty St., Box 4167, Metuchen, NJ 08840. (201-548-8600, 800-537-7107)

342. **Science Research Associates,** 155 N. Wacker Dr., Chicago, IL 60606. (312-984-7227, 800-621-0476)

343. **Scott Foresman,** 1900 E. Lake Ave., Glenview, IL 60025. (312-729-3000)

344. **Simon and Schuster,** 1230 Ave of the Americas, New York, NY 10020. (212-698-7000, 800-223-2348, 800-223-2336 orders)

345. **Society for Technical Communication,** 815 Fifteenth St. N.W., Washington, DC 20005. (202-737-0035, 619-746-4005 orders)

346. **South-Western Publishing Company,** 5101 Madison Rd., Cincinnati, OH 45227. (513-271-8811, 800-543-0487)

347. **Spon, E. and F. N.,** 11 New Fetter Lane, London, England EC4P 4EE, UK. (01-583-9855)

348. **Sterling Publishing Company,** 2 Park Ave., New York, NY 10016. (212-532-7160, 800-367-9692)

349. **Stipes Publishing Company,** P.O. Box 526, 10-12 Chester St., Champaign, IL 61820. (217-356-8391)

350. **Stuart, Lyle,** 120 Enterprise Ave., Secaucus, NJ 07094. (201-866-0490, 800-572-6657)

351. **Taplinger Publishing Company,** 132 W. Twenty-second St., New York, NY 10011. (212-877-1040)

352. **University of Michigan Press,** P.O. Box 1104, Ann Arbor, MI 48106. (313-764-4330, 313-764-4392 orders)

353. **Unwin Hyman,** 8 Winchester Pl., Winchester, MA 01890. (617-729-0830, 800-547-8889)

354. **Van Nostrand Reinhold,** 115 Fifth Ave., New York, NY 10003. (212-254-3232, 606-525-6600 orders)

355. **Vance Bibliographies,** P.O. Box 229, 112 N. Charter St., Monticello, IL 61856. (217-762-3831)

356. **Vanguard Press,** 424 Madison Ave., New York, NY 10017. (212-753-3906)

357. **Viking Penguin,** 40 W. Twenty-third St., New York, NY 10010. (212-337-5200, 800-631-3577)

358. **Wadsworth Publishing Company,** 10 Davis Dr., Belmont, CA 94002. (415-595-2350, 800-354-9706 orders)

359. **Washington Researchers,** 2612 P. St. N.W., Washington, DC 20007. (202-333-3533)

360. **Watts, Franklin,** 12A Golden Square, London, England W1R 4BA, UK. (01-437-0713)

361. **West Publishing,** P.O. Box 64526, 50 W. Kellogg Blvd., St. Paul, MN 55164. (612-228-2973, 800-328-9424, 800-328-2209 customer service)

362. **Wiley, John and Sons,** 605 Third Ave., New York, NY 10158. (212-850-6418, 800-526-5368)

RESEARCH INSTITUTIONS

363. **Center for Advanced Management Programs (CAMP).** University of Houston - Clear Lake, 2700 Bay Area Boulevard, Houston, TX 77058. (713-488-9533)

The center investigates organizational communication, stress, ethics, and advanced technologies management. There is an annual conference on managing advanced technology.

364. **Center for Communication Research.** Western Michigan University, Kalamazoo, MI 49001. (616-383-4089)

Interpersonal, small group, organizational and mass communication are examined. Research is issued in a semiannual publication.

365. **Center for Communication Research.** University of Wisconsin - Madison, 821 University Avenue, Madison, WI 53706. (608-263-3337)

This group performs research in interpersonal, small group and organizational communications.

366. **Center for Communication Studies.** Ohio University, Athens, OH 45701. (614-594-6118)

The center explores communicative processes and serves as a clearinghouse for special reports. Project reports are developed and short courses and seminars are taught on human communication behaviors and problems.

367. **Center for New Communications.** Indiana University, 200 Ernie Pyle Hall, Bloomington, IN 47405. (812-335-9247)

Various areas of journalism are studied such as newspaper design, effects of mass media and technology. Project and conference reports are produced. There are workshops and conferences at the center which has a sizable library.

368. **Center for the Study of Writing.** Division of Language and Literacy, School of Education, University of California - Berkeley, Berkeley, CA 94720. (415-643-7022)

Service training institutes are held for writing instructors.

369. **Center for the Study of Writing.** Miami University, Department of English, Oxford, OH 45056. (513-424-4444)

The writing process and its evaluation are the concern here. The Center issues a newsletter and sponsors a conference on the teaching of writing.

370. **Center for the Study of Writing and Literacy.** Education 127A, State University of New York at Albany, Albany, NY 12222. (518-442-5034)

The Center inquires into the writing process and the teaching of writing. Summer and in-service training institutes are held for writing instructors.

371. Communication Forum. University of Cincinnati, Cincinnati, OH 45221. (513-475-2551)

The forum studies group and media communication, speaking and listening strategies. It provides consulting and advisory services on specific problems of firms and government offices. There is a library of annual reports and videotapes are available.

372. Communication Research Center. Department of Communication, Arizona State University, Tempe, AZ 85287. (602-965-3774)

Research is conducted in interpersonal communication, communication effectiveness, organizational communication and group studies through surveys, studies and analyses. The Center holds monthly research colloquiums.

373. Communications Research Center. Brigham Young University, Department of Communications, E509 Harris Fine Arts Center, Provo, UT 84602. (801-378-7023)

The Center explores the areas of communication effectiveness in organizations, listening skills and interpersonal communications. It offers a series of occasional papers.

374. Communication Research Center. University of Florida, Gainesville, FL 32611. (904-392-6660)

Various areas are investigated such as mass media, organizational communication and interpersonal communications. Consulting and research services are available for mass media in Florida.

375. Communication Research Center. Office of Interdisciplinary Programs, Georgia Institute of Technology, Atlanta, GA 30332. (404-875-9200)

Writing research and faculty development are aided through instructional workshops and conferences. The Center is concerned with written literacy.

376. Communication Research Center. University of Kansas, 3090 Wescoe, Lawrence, KS 66045. (913-864-3633)

Communication problems in organizational and interpersonal communications are studied. The Center prepares papers, research reports and bibliographies from its research results.

377. Communication Research Laboratory. University of Iowa, 105 Communication Studies Building, Iowa City, IA 52240. (319-335-0579)

The Center directs experimental research into interpersonal, organizational and small group communicationss.

378. Communications Design Center. Carnegie-Mellon University, Baker Hall 160, Pittsburgh, PA 15213. (412-268-2906)

The Center concentrates on interdisciplinary research in the communication problems of business, industry and the professions. Procedures are developed for evaluating and improving business documents and computer documentation. A newsletter and technical reports are issued by the Center, which has its own library.

379. Department of Communication. Michigan State University, 474 Communication Arts, East Lansing, MI 48824. (517-355-3472)

The department considers areas of communication like the communication effectiveness of business organizations. Communications training is offered for government and private organizations.

380. Institute for Writing and Thinking. Bard College, 105 Ludlow, Annandale-on-Hudson, NY 12504. (914-758-6822)

The Institute publishes a series of papers with the results of its research on current writing theories and writing programs. There are conferences and workshops at high schools and colleges.

381. National Center for Business and Economic Communication. American University, 209 McCabe Building, 4400 Massachusetts Ave., N.W., Washington, DC 20016. (202-885-6167)

The Center's research in business and economic communication focuses on journalism education, current reporting practice and business and labor communications. It produces a monthly newsletter and holds seminars.

382. Reading and Learning Skills Center. University of Michigan, 1610 Washtenaw Avenue, Ann Arbor, MI 48104. (313-763-7195)

The Center conducts research on business and academic writing, reading, study and management skills. There are seminars for interns and staff, the Writer's Workshop and the annual North Central Reading Association Reading Conference. The facilities include a library on reading and behavior management.

383. Reading and Writing Center. University of Florida, 2109 Turlington Hall, Gainesville, FL 32611. (904-392-0791)

The Center operates separate reading and writing programs. Students are given assistance in developing skills through workshops on resume writing, writing essay exams, tests, study skills and other areas.

384. Reading Center. University of Pittsburgh, 5 H01 Forbes Quadrangle, Pittsburgh, PA 15260. (412-648-7298)

Listening, writing and oral language are studied with regard to language arts. Periodical reading/writing conferences and workshops/seminars are held for teachers. The Center's facilities include a language arts library.

385. Speech Communication Research Center. Texas Tech University, P.O. Box 4710, Lubbock, TX 79409. (806-742-2315)

The group fosters the study of organizational communication, speech comprehension and apprehension.

386. William T. Carter Foundation. 3700 Walnut Street, Philadelphia, PA 19104. (215-898-8130)

The foundation is concerned with reading, writing, oral communication, computers and reading. It sponsors intramural courses on child behavior and public lectures.

PART II

Communication Skills

Chapter 4

COMMUNICATION SKILLS

Communicating effectively with others requires skill. While mistakes are tolerated and can provoke humor in social situations, they produce misunderstandings and lost opportunities in the workplace. The successful business person communicates well with colleagues, subordinates, supervisors, and clients.

This chapter contains books with which general communication skills can be acquired and developed. The introductions to skill development found here fulfil the need for a basic review of writing and speaking skills. Two important abilities are grammar and style. Productive communication necessitates comprehension of the English language and adherence to its rules and forms. Both written documents and oral presentations demand correct grammar, punctuation and usage. There is a clearly recognizable writing style in business and technical documents. It is concise and to the point. While language can be enhanced by word choice and sentence construction, the type of informal writing permissable in correspondence between friends is inappropriate in business reports and technical manuals. The works cited here will help renew skills lost through disuse and develop strengths in new areas.

There are many ways to update little-used skills and acquire new ones. Described here are workbooks, programmed instruction texts, and author-devised learning systems. Workbooks offer exercises, questions, spaces for framing answers, and evaluation of responses. The programmed instruction texts are competency-based, requiring successful completion of sequential sections. Several books promote author-devised systems for the development of skills or written products. These can be found under the heading Writing Systems.

Written documents and oral presentations can be improved after initial production. Three skill areas assist that process: editing, graphics and word processing. Editing and revising skills rectify grammar, punctuation, usage, word choice, and other problems in one's own work or that of a colleague. Graphics and other visuals add clarity to printed documents and oral presentations. Charts, photographs or tables can explain results or functions in technical manuals and business reports. Word processing has become a survival skill in business and technical writing. General introductions to word processing use are included here. Those books which solve writing problems with a particular software; i.e., the writing of a business plan, are listed by application in Chapters 5 and 6.

EDITING AND REVISING

387. Arnold, Edmund C. *Editing the Organizational Publication*. Assisted by Kathleen A. Loomis. Chicago: Lawrence Ragan Communications, 1982. 283p.

Designed for those in journalism, this book describes the process of organizing and producing an organizational publication. Chapter headings are unclear, but the content, production and organization are discussed. Chapter three has the steps for creating a publication with a detailed production checklist. Indexed.

388. Chandler, Harry E. *Technical Writer's Handbook*. Metals Park, OH: American Society for Metals, 1983. 418p.

The results of a questionnaire are reported. Part two offers guidelines for writing and editing thirteen different formats of memos, letters, abstracts, summaries, proposals, reports, and other documents. There is a detailed table of contents. Indexed.

389. Lanham, Richard A. *Revising Business Prose*. 2d ed. New York: Macmillan; London: Collier Macmillan, 1987. 115p.

A quick method is shown for revising bureaucratese into plain English. The eight steps in the parametic method (PM) deal primarily with business style. Parts of speech and sentences are handled in the appendix. Not indexed.

390. Maki, Peggy, and Schilling, Carol. *Writing in Organizations*. New York: McGraw-Hill, 1987. 401p.

The authors focus on rhetoric, problem solving and critical thinking in written communication. Strategies, guidelines and checklists for editing and writing letters, procedural documents, proposals and reports are provided in a textbook format with examples, exercises and case studies. Indexed.

391. Minninger, Joan, and Putz, C. Delos Jr. *Writing Letters, Memos and Reports*. San Francisco: Workshops for Innovative Teaching, 1984. 194p.

A workbook on writing and rewriting techniques, this book uses before and after models. The techniques are applied to creating letters, memos, procedure manuals and reports, with blank worksheets for assignment completion. Not indexed.

392. *Proofreading Skills for Business*. New York: John Wiley and Sons, 1986. 194p.

Prepared by the staff of the Visual Education Corporation, it concerns the development of accurate proofreading skills. Numerous practical exercises support the discussion of basic skills such as the proofreading of numbers, common grammar, punctuation and spelling errors. It can be used for editing ones own or another's work. Indexed.

393. Ryckman, W. G. *What Do You Mean by That? The Art of Speaking and Writing Clearly.* Homewood, IL: Dow Jones-Irwin, 1980. 229p.

The basic techniques of oral and written communication are advanced. Practical methods, with useful hints and examples, are disclosed for presentations, writing style, editing, letters and reports. Not indexed.

394. Stratton, Charles R. *Technical Writing: Process and Product.* New York: Holt, Rinehart and Winston, 1984. 479p.

Writing and revising techniques for technical communications such as reports, letters, abstracts, proposals and manuals are given with many examples and some models of the shorter documents. The book also elaborates on writing for style and the editing of technical documents. Indexed.

395. Venolia, Jan. *Rewrite Right! How to Revise Your Way to Better Writing.* Berkeley, CA: Ten Speed Press, Periwinkle Press, 1987. 197p.

Communicates a practical approach to editing your writing and that of others. Editing of content, style, punctuation and grammar is considered with checklists, guidelines and examples. There are additional chapters on editing to eliminate bias, using word processing software such as spellcheckers, a glossary section and a separate list of lists. Indexed.

396. Visco, Louis J. *The Manager as an Editor: Reviewing Memos, Letters, and Reports.* Boston: CBI Publishing Company, 1981. 164p.

The author presents a systematic approach to editing the works of others in a clear, how-to manner. Chapter nine describes different kinds of documents. The editing guidelines could be used in writing and evaluating your own writing. Not indexed

397. Zimmerman, Donald E., and Clark, David G. *The Random House Guide to Technical and Scientific Communication.* New York: Random House, 1987. 451p.

While this is a basic textbook in technical writing, the strategies and guidelines in the application chapters are excellent. It elaborates on such areas as editing, presentations, letters, proposals, abstracts and reports. Additional references are provided. Indexed.

GENERAL COMMUNICATION SKILLS

398. Adelstein, Michael E., and Sparrow, W. Keats. *Business Communication.* New York: Harcourt Brace Jovanovich, 1983. 490p.

A textbook concerned with the development of oral and written communication skills, parts two through five reveal techniques for writing letters, memos and reports, and for planning and conducting presentations, interviews and meetings. There are many examples and models of letters, memos and the shorter reports. Appendix A is a glossary of business terminology. Indexed.

399. Beene, Lynn, and White, Peter, eds. *Solving Problems in Technical Writing.* New York: Oxford University Press, 1988. 241p.

Volume unavailable for examination.

400. Bogert, Judith B. W., and Worley, Rebecca B. *Managing Business Communications. An Applied Process Approach*. Englewood Cliffs, NJ: Prentice-Hall, 1988. 434p.

This business communications textbook focuses on the communication process rather than specific types of documents. It contains information on writing skills, style and listening. Chapters have examples, among which are models of an executive summary and a report. Chapter fifteen discusses developing a presentation. Editing and letter formats are handled in the appendices. The handbook of letter and report types is an alphabetical encyclopedia which defines types of communication such as abstracts and proposals. Indexed.

401. Fallon, William K., ed. *Effective Communication on the Job*. 3d ed. New York: AMACOM, 1981. 328p.

The series of thirty-six essays deals with communication on the job. New readings are supplemented by three from the previous edition and reprints from periodicals. The essays selected combine theoretical approaches to the topic with more practical ones. This could function as supplemental reading or a review of research. Indexed.

402. Locker, Kitty O. *Business and Administrative Communication*. Homewood, IL: Irwin, 1989. 652p.

Volume unavailable for examination.

403. Pickett, Nell A., and Laster, Ann A. *Technical English: Writing, Reading, and Speaking*. 4th ed. New York: Harper and Row, 1984. 722p.

The three-part book combines the principles of communication with selected illustrative readings and a handbook of grammar and usage. The application chapters show summaries, letters, memos and reports using models and excercise plan sheets. Indexed.

404. Rader, Martha H., and Kurth, Linda A. *Business Communication for the Computer Age*. Cincinnati, OH: South-Western Publishing Company, 1988. 578p.

Volume unavailable for examination.

405. Redding, W. Charles. *The Corporate Manager's Guide to Better Communication*. Glenview, IL: Scott Foresman, 1984. 157p.

A nine-step approach is presented for improving general communications abilities. Aimed at corporate managers, guidance and detailed checklists are introduced for improving skills in perceiving, listening, reading, writing and speaking. Reference is made to other volumes in the series for more practical information. Indexed.

406. Rietmann, Kearney. *Language from Nine to Five: Developing Business Communication Skills*. Englewood Cliffs, NJ: Prentice-Hall, 1985. 161p.

The twenty-six sociodrama lessons contained in the volume promote practice in vocabulary, listening, roleplaying, oral communication and written communication skills. There is a useful glossary. Not indexed.

407. Sorrels, Bobbye D. *Business Communication Fundamentals*. Columbus, OH: Charles E. Merrill, 1984. 584p.

This textbook concentrates on refining written messages (letters, memos, reports), developing receiving skills (listening, reading) and speaking effectively (interviews, speeches, television, radio) for business communications. Chapters include examples, samples, tests and vocabulary. There are nineteen reading self tests with answers. Indexed.

408. Spitzer, Michael; Gamble, Michael W.; and Gamble, Teri K. *Writing and Speaking in Business*. New York: Random House, 1984. 340p.

The learning system emphasizes strategies and appropriate learning experinces in a textbook format. Both written and oral forms such as letters, memos, reports and oral presentations are considered. Models of written forms are indicated in the index. Frequently confused words and avoiding sexist language are covered in the appendices. Indexed.

409. Stallard, John J.; Smith, E. Ray; and Price, Sandra F. *Business Communication: A Strategic Approach*. Homewood, IL: Irwin, 1989. 705p.

Volume unavailable for examination.

410. Timm, Paul R. *Managerial Communication: A Finger on the Pulse*. 2d ed. Englewood Cliffs, NJ: Prentice-Hall, 1986. 397p.

Basic oral and written communication skills are presented within an organizational context. Meant for managers, practical applications are advanced for skill development in meetings, listening, presentations, letters, memos and reports. Chapter twelve has guidelines for diagnosing specific communication skills in an organization. Indexed.

411. Wells, Gordon. *How to Communicate*. 2d ed. London: McGraw-Hill, 1986. 190p.

This is an introduction to the principles of effective writing, speaking, listening and reading in a business context. The principles are applied, with checklists and some guidelines, to letters, press releases, reports, speeches, interviews and meetings. It includes discussion of the use of word processing and electronic mail. Indexed.

412. Wilkinson, C. W.; Wilkinson, Dorothy C.; and Vik, Gretchen N. *Communicating Through Writing and Speaking in Business*. 9th ed. Homewood, IL: Richard D. Irwin, 1986. 683p.

A revised edition of *Communicating Through Letters and Reports* (1983), the textbook stresses the development of written and oral skills. Letters, memos, resumes, listening, interviews, presentations and reports are covered. The book has checklists (which also appeared in the 1983 edition), examples and some sample documents (with samples indicated in the index and table of contents). The appendices include cases and a handbook on grammar and usage. Indexed.

GRAMMAR, PUNCTUATION AND USAGE

413. Bachman, Lois J.; Sigband, Norman B.; and Hipple, Theodore W. *Successful Business English*. 2d ed. Glenview, IL: Scott Foresman, 1987. 496p.

Designed in a workbook format, the authors seek to sharpen communication skills in business situations. Students and practitioners can use the book to review the basics for parts of speech, sentences, punctuation and capitalization. Applications are briefly covered, with some sample documents as textual examples. Indexed.

414. Barry, Robert E. *Business English for the 80's*. Englewood Cliffs, NJ: Prentice-Hall, 1980. 424p.

Grammar, punctuation, usage, spelling and dictionary study are practiced in a workbook format. Designed for undergraduates, the pretest and answer key promote use as a self-teaching guide by anyone needing to communicate more effectively. A new edition, *Business English for the 90's*, was due for publication in 1988. Indexed.

415. Bielawski, Larry, and Parks, A. Franklin. *Organizational Writing*. Belmont, CA: Wadsworth Publishing Company, 1987. 535p.

The writing process and strategies for developing letters, memos, proposals, reports and presentations are disclosed in this organizational writing textbook. The authors provide checklists and samples of written documents; a handbook of grammar, punctuation and mechanics; and a glossary of usage. Indexed.

416. Bromage, Mary C. *Writing for Business*. 2d ed. Ann Arbor, MI: University of Michigan Press, 1980. 178p.

This is a basic guide to purposeful writing for students and practitioners. It should be used in conjunction with a grammar manual. While the emphasis is on usage, chapter four covers specific formats and has a model of a long report. There is an appendix on sentence building. Indexed.

417. Carbone, Mary T. *Modern Business English: A Systems Approach*. Boston: PWS-Kent Publishing Company, 1988. 305p.

Volume unavailable for examination.

418. Cullinan, Mary P. *Business English for Industry and the Professions*. Chicago: Dryden Press, 1987. 570p.

The English grammar and usage textbook was designed for students in business and industry. Practical applications are emphasized, particularly for editing and writing memos and resumes. A useful glossary of grammatical and editing terms is in the appendices. Indexed.

419. Fear, David E. *Technical Communication*. 2d ed. Glenview, IL: Scott Foresman, 1981. 385p.

Communications theory is applied to creating memos, letters, reports and oral presentations. Checklists, examples and models are available; however, the models appear as figures in the text and can't be located through the index. Part three consists of a handbook for review of grammar, punctuation and usage. Indexed.

420. Grossman, Carol. *Business English Simplified and Self-Taught*. New York: Arco Publishing, 1982. 138p.

A self-teaching approach, students are acquainted with the usage, punctuation, sentences and related skills. Chapter five deals with letters and chapter ten with oral communication. The answers are available for part of the review exercises. Indexed.

421. Guffey, Mary Ellen. *Business English*. 2d ed. Boston, MA: Kent Publishing Company, 1986. 356p.

The English usage textbook for business students introduces basic principles, nouns, verbs, modifyers and punctuation. Exercises (with blank worksheets) are arranged in three levels of difficulty. The appendices cover related issues of spelling, vocabulary, formats, argumentative and expository writing. Indexed.

422. Henderson, Greta L., and Voiles, Price R. *Business English Essentials*. 7th ed. New York: McGraw-Hill, 1987. 302p.

Basically this is a textbook on the fundamentals of English grammar and usage with practice exercises and worksheets (without answers). Part four addresses letters primarily and memos and reports briefly. The index is located in the front of the book. Indexed.

423. Keithley, Erwin M., and Thompson, Margaret H. *English for Modern Business*. 5th ed. Homewood, IL: Richard D. Irwin, 1986. 416p.

The development of English usage skills is the concern here. The textbook emphasizes practice through writing with words, sentences and paragraphs. Indexed.

424. Lane, Gloria. *Project Text for Executive Communication*. San Diego, CA: Lane and Associates, 1980. 92p.

The basic review of grammar and English usage for executives has some excercises, blank workbook pages and examples. Written communication is stressed through brief discussion of letters, memos and reports. There is one chapter on oral presentations. The lack of either an index or a table of contents makes use difficult and effectively hides the word lists in the appendices. Not indexed.

425. Neufeld, Jacqueline K. *A Handbook for Technical Communication*. Englewood Cliffs, NJ: Prentice-Hall, 1987. 214p.

The textbook for students of English as a second language reviews usage and writing skills. There are several applications chapters. Model documents appear in the application chapters on letters, memos, proposals and reports. Not indexed.

426. Paxson, William C. *The Mentor Guide to Punctuation. A New, Easy-to-Use System*. New York: New American Library, 1986. 212p.

The concise punctuation handbook begins with the purpose of a punctuation mark rather than a grammatical rule. American punctuation practice as seen in the popular press is advanced with clear instructions and examples. The author has included a glossary of terms used in the book. Indexed.

427. Pryse, B. Elizabeth. *Successful Communication in Business*. Oxford: Basil Blackwell, 1981. 262p.

This book considers specific methods for solving communications problems in eight areas of commerce. Vocabulary, techniques and exercises for mastering the use of the English language are offered. There is a general glossary and a glossary for each area of commerce discussed. Some models of letters and reports can be found in the text as well as the answers for the self-teaching practice questions. Indexed.

428. Romine, Jack S.; Hanson, Ladine; and Holdridge, Thelma. *College Business English*. 4th ed. Englewood Cliffs, NJ: Prentice-Hall, 1988. 366p.

Volume unavailable for examination.

429. Schimmel, Warren T., and Camp, Carolyn B. *Communicating*. New York: John Wiley and Sons, 1987. 624p.

The communications textbook stresses the development of grammar and usage skills. The reader is acquainted with the writing of letters, memos and resumes. There are examples but no sample documents. Listening, speaking, reading and telephone skills are discussed as well. Indexed.

430. Sherman, Theodore A., and Johnson, Simon S. *Modern Technical Writing*. 4th ed. Englewood Cliffs, NJ: Prentice-Hall, 1983. 499p.

Technical writing skills are applied to writing letters, proposals, reports and preparing presentations. In this textbook the models are indicated in the index. Part four functions as a handbook of grammar and usage, with a glossary. Indexed.

431. Smithson, Sue. *Business Communication Today: A Guide to Effective Communication Techniques*. Cambridge: ICSA Publishing, 1984. 232p.

This guide to effective communication techniques briefly describes the application of communication skills to such job-related problems as reports, letters, oral presentation, meetings and interviews. Models of written forms appear as textual figures. Part five contains instructions on parts of speech, syntax, vocabulary and presentation. Indexed.

432. Sorenson, Sharon. *Webster's New World Student Writing Handbook*. New York: Webster's New World, Prentice-Hall, 1988. 589p.

Volume unavailable for examination.

433. Taintor, Sarah A. and Monro, Kate M. *The Secretary's Handbook*. 10th ed. New York: Macmillan; London: Collier Macmillan, 1988. 422p.

A handbook for secretaries, the authors underscore the importance of grammar and usage skills. The chapters on letters and reports have sample documents such as a sample letter of transmittal. Forms of address and the useful skills of proofreading, indexing and creating a bibliography are shown. An extensive list of sources of information is in chapter twenty-five. Indexed.

434. Thomas, David A., and Fryar, Maridell. *Business Communication Today*. Edited by Barbara Blunk. Lincolnwood, IL: National Textbook Company, 1984. 486p.

The basics of oral and written communication are presented in this textbook with review questions and exercises. There is a lengthy handbook of grammar and usage. Indexed.

435. Turner, Maxine T. *Technical Writing: A Practical Approach*. Reston, VA: Reston Publishing Company, 1984. 507p.

After introducing technical writing, the book describes and examines the major forms of communication. A problem-solving approach to letters, memos, proposals, presentations and several kinds of reports is used with many examples and samples. Part four is a handbook of grammar and usage. The appendices furnish suggestions for writing to specification and evaluation checklists. Indexed.

436. Wolf, Morris P. *Effective Communication in Business*. 8th ed. Cincinnati, OH: South-Western Publishing Company, 1984. 485p.

This textbook employs a process approach to business communication concepts and methods. The chapters supply students with discussion questions, exercises and case studies. Basic messages, reports and the oral presention are investigated, with sample documents listed in the abbreviations list. Part eight is a review of grammar and usage. Indexed.

GRAPHICS AND VISUALS

437. Lefferts, Robert. *Elements of Graphics: How to Prepare Charts and Graphs for Effective Reports*. New York: Harper and Row, 1981. 166p.

Preparing charts and other graphics for inclusion in reports can be accomplished easily with this practical, how-to guide. Basic principles and step-by-step examples illustrate the process. Chapter twelve reports on equipment and materials. This book is also available in soft cover under the title *How to Prepare Charts and Graphs for Effective Reports*. Indexed.

438. Zelazny, Gene. *Say it with Charts. The Executive's Guide to Successful Presentations*. Homewood, IL: Dow Jones-Irwin, 1985. 130p.

This book offers guidelines on choosing and using charts for presentations with exercises and their solutions. Part two has a portfolio of sample charts. Indexed.

ORAL COMMUNICATION SKILLS

439. Arthur, Richard. *The Engineer's Guide to Better Communication*. Glenview, IL: Scott Foresman, 1984. 125p.

The brief overview of communication principles and applications for technologically-oriented writers highlights oral communication. Part of a series, it includes examples in the text. Indexed.

440. Berko, Roy M.; Wolvin, Andrew D.; and Wolvin, Darlyn R. *Communicating: A Social and Career Focus*. 3d ed. Boston: Houghton Mifflin, 1985. 421p.

The authors combine communication theory with instructions for development of listening, interviewing and presentation skills. The book provides practical advice, examples and sample outlines. Indexed.

441. Bormann, Ernest G., et al. *Interpersonal Communication in the Modern Organization*. 2d ed. Englewood Cliffs, NJ: Prentice-Hall, 1982. 287p.

While the first edition was aimed at professionals, the second edition has been adapted for use as a textbook, with the addition of classroom assignments and laboratory applications. Primarily concerned with organizational communications, several useful chapters discuss listening, making presentations, and meetings. The applications chapters use key features or checklists in moving from simpler to the more complex communications needs of upper management. Indexed.

442. Fellows, Hugh, and Ikeda, Fusaye. *Business Speaking and Writing*. Englewood Cliffs, NJ: Prentice-Hall, 1982. 366p.

This introduction to business speaking and writing for students highlights oral communication. The practical approach, exercises, vocabulary study and examples can be easily put to use. Model letters appear in chapters eighteen and nineteen. Indexed.

443. Kaumeyer, Richard A. Jr. *How to Write and Speak in Business*. New York: Van Nostrand Reinhold, 1985. 125p.

The book concentrates on skill development in writing and speaking in such areas as meetings, memos, reports and presentations. Sample documents appear for memos only. The advantages and disadvantages of different kinds of media are debated. Indexed.

444. Lewis, David V. *Secrets of Successful Writing, Speaking, and Listening*. New York: AMACOM, 1982. 188p.

Basic coverage of written and oral communication skills comprises this volume. Practical tips are offered on correspondence, speeches and meetings, with pertinent examples. Indexed.

445. Makay, John J., and Fetzer, Ronald C. *Business Communication Skills: Principles and Practice*. 2d ed. Englewood Cliffs, NJ: Prentice-Hall, 1984. 282p.

Communications theory and practical guidance for the development of communications skills are considered with examples and instructional activities. Oral communication skills reported are presentations, telephone behavior, interviews, meetings, listening, and conferences. Each chapter contains a review of key issues. Indexed.

446. Munter, Mary. *Guide to Managerial Communication*. 2d ed. Englewood Cliffs, NJ: Prentice-Hall, 1987. 168p.

Communications theories, with practical advice on writing, speaking and format, are advanced in moving from process to product. Techniques and procedures are explained; useful checklists and numerous examples are provided. The reference section contains definitions, usage, punctuation, and bibliography. Indexed.

447. Murphy, Herta A., and Hildebrandt, Herbert W. *Effective Business Communication.* 4th ed. New York: McGraw-Hill, 1984. 737p.

The development of organizational, analytical, writing and speaking skills is the concern of this textbook. Guidelines, checklists and examples are disclosed for effective letters, memos, reports, presentation, meetings and interviews. The checklists are listed separately in the table of contents. Appendix B reinforces skills in language mechanics and writing style. Indexed.

448. Rasberry, Robert W., and Lemoine, Laura F. *Effective Managerial Communication.* Boston: Kent Publishing Company, 1986. 484p.

This managerial communications textbook advances the techniques and principles of organizational communication and applies them to listening, presentations, meetings, interviewing, and written documents. Along with many textual examples, eight speeches and models of letters, memos and reports are provided in the appendices. Chapter sixteen summarizes the major points covered in the text. Indexed.

449. Vervalin, Charles H., ed. *Communication and the Technical Professional.* Houston, TX: Gulf Publishing Company, 1981. 138p.

Communication skills, such as listening, speaking and meetings, are the focus of this series of readings. The articles, which stress skill development, vary in length and practicality. This is best used in combination with a textbook. Not indexed.

450. Weaver, Richard L., II. *Understanding Business Communication.* Englewood Cliffs, NJ: Prentice-Hall, 1985. 372p.

With an emphasis on the development of oral communication skills, each chapter of this business communication textbook is a self-contained unit. Listening, interviewing, resumes, meetings, presentations, letters, memos and reports (oral and written) are presented. There is a glossary of related terms. Indexed.

STYLE

451. Barkas, J. L. *How to Write Like a Professional.* New York: Arco Publishing, 1985. 163p.

This book is a compact guide for the beginner to nonfiction writing. The basics of style, content and writing of professional letters are displayed. Indexed.

452. Henze, Geraldine. *From Murk to Masterpiece: Style for Business Writing.* Homewood, IL: Richard D. Irwin, 1984. 103p.

Focusing on the development of style in business writing, three chapters form a guide to the editing of stylistic weaknesses. There is a bibliography and glossary of grammaticaal terms in the appendices. Not indexed.

453. Himstreet, William C., and Baty, Wayne M. *Business Communications: Principles and Methods*. 8th ed. Boston: Kent Publishing Company, 1987. 629p.

The development of oral and written communication skills are stressed with exercises, case studies and numerous models. Language style is applied to letters, memos, proposals and reports. Three oral skills are discussed: listening, interviews and presentations. The text elaborates on intercultural communication and word processing. The appendices include a pretest and brief coverage of grammar. Indexed.

454. Lyon, David G. *The XYZ's of Business Writing*. New York: Dembner Books, 1986. 80p.

The author briefly presents general writing principles and guidelines. The concern is with writing style rather than any specific form. Eleven keys to good writing appear directly before the appendix. Indexed.

455. Newman, Ruth G.; Danziger, Marie A.; and Cohen, Mark. *Communicating in Business Today*. Lexington, MA: D.C. Heath, 1987. 626p.

After introducing communication strategies, four case study dialogues are used to teach oral and written business communication skills. Problem-solving solutions are furnished for writing letters, memos, report; preparing oral presentations; and planning meetings. One dialogue is concerned with writing with style. This apprach employs seven selected readings within the text. Indexed.

456. Olson, Gary A.; De George, James; and Ray, Richard. *Style and Readability in Business Writing*. New York: Random House, 1985. 212p.

A sentence-combining approach is utilized to produce clear, economical, readable writing. Unit eleven shows sentence-combining exercises in letters, memos, abstracts and reports. This is a textbook with a brief glossary and is indexed by topic and exercise format. Indexed.

457. Paxson, William C. *Principles of Style for the Business Writer*. New York: Dodd, Mead and Company, 1985. 162p.

The principles of business style in writing are combined with a discussion of usage, sentences, paragraphs and grammar. The book is aimed at achieving clear business prose. Indexed.

458. Price, Jonathan. *Put That in Writing*. New York: Viking Penguin, 1984. 209p.

The book begins with a discussion of style and basic writing skills and proceeds to brief guidelines on developing memos, letters, proposals, reports, speeches, employee reviews and different kinds of manuals. Examples of the shorter written documents are included. Indexed.

459. Roundy, Nancy. *Strategies for Technical Communication*. Written with David Mair. Boston: Little, Brown and Company, 1985. 421p.

This technical writing textbook focuses on the writing process. Case studies, checklists and samples are used to illustrate the process whereby memos, letters, proposals and reports are created. Part five is a handbook of style and includes grammar, punctuation and usage. Indexed.

460. Swindle, Robert E., and Swindle, Elizabeth M. *The Business Communicator.* 2d ed. Englewood Cliffs, NJ: Prentice-Hall, 1985. 562p.

Communication theory is presented and applied to specific kinds of written and oral communication. The authors provide checklists and samples of letters, memos, resumes and a short report. Within oral communication, meetings, speeches, interviews and telephone usage are described. Grammar, punctuation and usage appear in the appendices; style is in part two. A new edition is to be published in 1989. Indexed.

461. Turk, Christopher, and Kirkman, John. *Effective Writing: Improving Scientific, Technical and Business Communication.* London: E. and F. N. Spon, 1982. 257p.

The book combines a discussion of basic communication principles with practical guidance on the selection, organization and presentation of information. Emphasis is on written communication and style in letters, summaries and reports. The appendices consider a formula for readability and the electronic office. A new edition is scheduled for publication in 1988. Indexed.

462. Weeks, Francis W.; Jameson, Daphne A.; and Gieselman, Robert D. *Principles of Business Communication.* 3d ed. Champaign, IL: Stipes Publishing Company, 1984. 193p.

The authors offer principles and techniques for improving writing style. These are applied to reports, abstracts and other documents in general terms. The references at the end of each chapter lead to more practical how-to-do-it books. Useful outlines are located in the companion volume on cases and problems by Kitty Locker. Not indexed.

WORD PROCESSING

463. Brown, Eric D. *Throw Away Your Pencil: Writing More Effectively with a Word Processor.* Reston, VA: Reston Publishing Company, 1984. 136p.

Designed to increase writing skills through the use of word processing, the book stresses planning, rewriting, and the potential of word processing. It does not describe how to use a word processor. The writing of business letters is covered with examples. Indexed.

464. Holtz, Herman. *Word Processing for Business Publications.* New York: McGraw-Hill, 1985. 289p.

The selection of word processing equipment and its application in the production of business documents is contained in this volume. The general approach is not as useful as books on desktop publishing or the preparation of specific kinds of document through word processing. There is a glossary and list of vendors. Indexed.

465. Institute of Financial Education. *In Plain Words. A Guide to Financial Services Writing*. Chicago, 1984. 334p.

Developed from the Institute's business writing course, this is a textbook on writing for financial institutions. After a discussion of general writing principles, the chapters deal with specific applications such as letters and reports. Guidelines and many examples are included. Chapter ten on word processing is good. Indexed.

466. King, Patricia. *Mind to Disk to Paper. Business Writing on a Word Processor*. New York: Franklin Watts, 1984. 139p.

The author concisely introduces better writing, use of word processing equipment, and specific kinds of reports. The chapters reveal suggested formats, guidelines and standards. There is a glossary of related terms. Indexed.

467. Krull, Robert, ed. *Word Processing for Technical Writers*. Amityville, NY: Baywood Publishing Company, 1988. 172p.

The collection of eleven essays will help writers use word processing effectively. Part two investigates organizing, creating outlines and editing through spellchecker and grammar checker. Part three acquaints readers with graphics and electronic publishing capabilities. Not indexed.

468. Pfaffenberger, Bryan. *Business Communication in the Personal Computer Age*. Homewood, IL: Irwin, 1987. 170p.

This introduction to the use of word processing in business writing explains how to use any word processing program well. While it emphasizes general concepts, several chapters describe letters, reports and graphics with examples. Such areas as choosing a word processing system and conducting business research are considered. The book has a glossary of terms. Indexed.

469. Quible, Zane K.; Johnson, Margaret H.; and Mott, Dennis L. *Introduction to Business Communication*. Englewood Cliffs, NJ: Prentice-Hall, 1981. 435p.

Based on the author's teaching experience, a pragmatic approach to the mastery of communication skills is furnished. Written communication, with examples of letters and reports, the specialized applications disclosed are press releases, editorials, meetings, word processing and oral presentations. The appendices cover several aspects of grammar and usage. Indexed.

470. Robbins, Jane E., and Curtin, Dennis P. *Contemporary Business Letters with Wordstar*. Somerville, MA: Curtin and London; New York: Van Nostrand Reinhold, 1983. 227p.

The use of Wordstar in the creation, editing and mailing of correspondence is presented. The authors explain using form letters (with samples) and creating individualized letters. Reveals, in detail, how to use Wordstar for revising and formatting letters, and the mailmerge feature for direct mail marketing. The table of contents notes pages with word processing tips. Indexed.

471. Segal, Arthur M. *Business Writing Using Word Processing Apple Writer Edition*. New York: John Wiley and Sons, 1987. 131p.

Word processing techniques that are useful for the improvement writing skills are introduced. The techniques are demonstrated for constructing better letters, memos, proposals and reports. Part two explores beginning, intermediate and advanced use of Apple Writer. Error messages are in the appendix. Indexed.

472. Segal, Arthur M. *Business Writing Using Word Processing: IBM Easywriter Edition.* New York: John Wiley and Sons, 1987. 141p.

A similar approach is employed by the author in fabricating letters, memos, proposals and reports with IBM EasyWriter. Error messages are in the appendix. Indexed.

473. Segal, Arthur M. *Business Writing Using Word Processing: IBM Wordstar Edition.* New York: John Wiley and Sons, 1987. 141p.

Part one is the same as others in the series. Part two has instructions on use of IBM Wordstar. Standard error messages are in the appendix. Indexed.

WORKBOOKS AND PROGRAMMED INSTRUCTION

474. Aldrich, Pearl G. *How to Plan and Organize Your Writing.* Washington, DC: Research Enterprises Publications, 1985. 81p.

Developed from the author's executive writing workshop, this workbook implements the author's method for learning to write more effectively. Requiring four to six hours for completion, it leads the reader through three basic steps: planning, focusing, and organizing. Exercises and models are part of the workbook. Not indexed.

475. Christen, William L.; Stoll, Richard T.; and Goodsell, Karen F. *Strategies in Business Communications.* Englewood Cliffs, NJ: Prentice-Hall, 1981. 192p.

Strategies are advanced for forming letters, memos, resumes and short reports. This is basically a textbook which uses a workbook-like arrangement for exercises (with answers in the appendix). There is a glossary and review of punctuation in the appendices. Indexed.

476. Delaware Technical and Community College, Southern Campus. *Writing Skills for Technical Students.* 2d ed. Written collectively by Sara D. Lewis et al. Englewood Cliffs, NJ: Prentice-Hall, 1988. 356p.

The self-paced, modularized program on writing skills for adult learners stresses grammar instruction. Individual modules are devoted to reports and letters. Besides activities, planning forms, outlines, guidelines and examples are given for reports, memos, letters and resumes. A blank progress form is included for students. Indexed.

477. Dumaine, Deborah. *Write to the Top: Writing for Corporate Success.* New York: Random House, 1983. 141p.

This approach to writing was developed from on-site workshops. It promotes guidance and practice in organization, style, sentence construction, usage and grammar. A self-paced, individualized approach is used with answers in the appendix. Not indexed.

478. Georges, T. M. *Business and Technical Writing Cookbook: How to Write Coherently on the Job*. Boulder, CO: Syntax Publications, 1983. 244p.

Practice is emphasized, and grammatical rules and communications theory are avoided in this workbook on writing improvement. Concentrating on skill development, procedures are organized in a step-by-step manner. Chapter eight has checklists for specific documents such as proposals, manuals, reports and correspondence. Indexed.

479. Guffey, Mary E. *Essentials of Business Communication. A Writing Improvement Program*. Boston: PWS-Kent Publishing Company, 1988. 363p.

A business communication textbook, the workbook format instructs students in both written and oral communication. The text considers memos, letters, reports, resumes, listening and oral reports. Examples, application exercises and samples (letters, memos, memo reports and resumes) are offered. There is a very useful grammar and mechanics review handbook. Indexed.

480. Hemphill, Phyllis D. *Business Communications With Writing Improvement Exercises*. 3d ed. Englewood Cliffs, NJ: Prentice-Hall, 1986. 328p.

The workbook develops oral and written communication skills through the provision of useful checklists, review questions and chapter worksheets. Guidelines for creating letters, memos and reports are a welcome addition. Questions about punctuation and spelling rules are answered in the appendices. Indexed.

481. Londo, Richard J. *Common Sense in Business Writing*. New York: Macmillan; London: Collier Macmillan, 1982. 470p.

The fundamental and advanced writing techniques presented here are applied to letters and reports. Chapters include tests and answers. English usage is reviewed briefly. Indexed.

482. Mehaffy, Robert E. *Writing for the Real World*. Glenview, IL: Scott Foresman, 1980. 376p.

The self-paced exercises communicate basic technical writing terminology and techniques. Concepts are followed by examples and an exercise. Chapters have objectives and checklists for letters, memos and an informal report. Answers to the exercises are in the appendix. Indexed.

483. Messer, Ronald K. *Style in Technical Writing: A Text/Workbook*. Glenview, IL: Scott Foresman, 1982. 226p.

The author gives the seven principles of effective technical writing style. Based on the author's consulting business, the workbook helps students add style to their technical writing. The appendices review words and expressions. There is a glossary. Indexed.

484. Michulka, Jean H. *Let's Talk Business*. 3d ed. Cincinnati, OH: South-Western Publishing Company, 1988. 370p.

The communications textbook combines a description of communication skills with practical individual and group activities. Each chapter has a checklist of communications terms and concludes with a workshop of activities and forms to complete. Oral skills are highlighted through listening, speaking and presentations. Indexed.

485. Moyer, Ruth. *Business English Basics: A Programmed Approach*. New York: John Wiley and Sons, 1980. 568p.

This book is a self-paced instructional workbook on the study of English fundamentals. The many examples are business-related ones. Grammar, usage, punctuation and spelling form an important part of the workbook. Indexed.

486. Quattrini, Joseph A. *Brushing Up Your Writing Skills*. New York: Arco Publishing, 1985. 246p.

Techniques for the improvement of writing are implemented in a self-instructional guide. Practical exercises support learning with evaluation and punctuation guides. The workbook also has a guide to spelling and word division. Not indexed.

487. Robinson, Patricia A. *Fundamentals of Technical Writing*. Boston: Houghton Mifflin, 1985. 299p.

The technical writing textbook views writing as a design problem. The workbooks' chapters require the planning and evaluating of written documents, such as letters and reports, and presentations. The separate grammar, usage and mechanics handbook is useful. A sample report appears in the appendix. Indexed.

488. Sigband, Norman B. *Business Communication*. With the assistance of Susan R. Pollack. San Diego, CA: Harcourt Brace Jovanovich, 1984. 157p.

Part of a college outline series, this work presents business communication in an outline form. The chapters consist of definitions, basic elements, questions, summary, rapid review section and problems (with answers). The communication skills outlined are letters, resumes, reports, annual report, presentations, listening, meetings and interviews. Among the examples are samples of letters, memos and resumes. Meant to accompany a textbook, it can be used for independent study as well. The glossary, midterm and final exams (with answers) should prove valuable. Indexed.

489. Timm, Paul R.; Young, Ray L.; and Jones, Christopher G. *Basic Business English and Communication*. Englewood Cliffs, NJ: Prentice-Hall, 1986. 379p.

The authors emphasize skill development while explaining the use of mechanics, style and the psychology of business writing. The workbook develops letters, memos, reports, listening, presentation and resume skills. Model documents are indicated in the table of contents. Indexed.

490. Warner, Joan E. *Business English for Careers*. abr. ed. Reston, VA: Reston Publishing Company, 1984. 374p.

This volume reviews grammar, spelling, punctuation, sentences, vocabulary and editing. Career language skills are discovered in thirty lessons, with an answer key. Indexed.

WRITING SKILLS

491. Alvarez, Joseph A. *The Elements of Technical Writing*. New York: Harcourt Brace Jovanovich, 1980. 208p.

Fifty axioms on major writing problem areas are advanced. Students and professionals are challenged to write clearly and concisely. Designed as both a guide to technical writing and a reference guide, the book discloses the elements of writing such as words, sentences, punctuation, format and style within the framework of communicating technical information. Four appendices add to its usefulness. Indexed.

492. Andrews, William D., and Andrews, Deborah C. *Write for Results*. Boston: Little, Brown and Company, 1982. 113p.

Designed as a quick read for professionals, this is a practical guide to improving written communication. Developed from the authors' teaching experience, it contains advice on the planning process and specific guidelines (and examples) for writing summaries, memos, letters, proposals and reports. The index and list of figures can be used to locate the model documents. Indexed.

493. Aronoff, Craig E., et al. *Getting Your Message Across*. St. Paul, MN: West Publishing, 1981. 411p.

Communication skills are developed through an understanding of the process in this book. Identified principles are applied to the writing of letters, memos, reports and the development of presentations and listening skills. The appendices supply a handbook of grammar, punctuation and spelling. Indexed.

494. Bacon, Mark S. *Write Like the Pros*. New York: John Wiley and Sons, 1988. 316p.

Five professional rules of writing are investigated. The book introduces professional writing ideas and techniques for letters, proposals, memos and reports. There are models of the shorter formats. A how-to system for putting the book to work can be found in the appendix. This should be read first. Indexed.

495. Baird, John W., and Stull, James B. *Business Communication: Strategies and Solutions*. New York: McGraw-Hill, 1983. 426p.

The problem-solving method used combines communications theory with practice in oral and written communication. The text concentrates on communications which tell something, sell something and resolve problems. Of particular interest are the example-filled sections on letters, memos, reports and presentations. A sample report and checklist are in the appendix. Indexed.

496. Bakos, Brian D. *Business Communications at Work*. Englewood Cliffs, NJ: Prentice-Hall, 1988. 239p.

Development of business communication skills is the premise of this textbook. Written skills are highlighted through consideration of style, memos, letters, resumes and reports. Exercises (with workbook pages) and samples of letters, memos and a resume are available. The exercises become progressively more difficult. A short glossary and brief review of punctuation are in the appendix. Indexed.

497. Batteiger, Richard P. *Business Writing: Process and Forms*. Belmont, CA: Wadsworth Publishing Company, 1985. 467p.

This is a skill development textbook. The writing process and writing strategies are reviewed with particular attention to letters, memos, proposals and reports. One chapter discusses listening and oral presentations. The appendices offer editing, sample letters (Appendix B), formats, legal issues and word processing. Indexed.

498. Bell, Arthur H. *A Way With Words: Effective Writing Techniques for the Business Professional*. Brentwood, NY: Asher-Gallant Press, 1988. 129p.

Volume unavailable for examination.

499. Bell, Arthur H., and Wyse, Roger. *The One-Minute Business Writer*. Homewood, IL: Dow Jones-Irwin, 1987. 194p.

Business writing practice is simplified into sixty one-minute lessons. The short, practical, how-to lessons cover pre-writing, drafting, revising and applying. There are separate sections on grammar and usage and sample business documents. An index speeds access to the most common errors and areas needing improvement. Indexed.

500. Blicq, Ron S. *Technically-Write! Communicating in a Technological Era*. 3d ed. Englewood Cliffs, NJ: Prentice-Hall, 1986. 411p.

Using a case-study approach, the book introduces technicians and technical managers to problem solving in typical communication situations. Unlike other works in technical writing, it begins with the writing of specific documents before it covers the writing proces. Each chapter has assignments of varying complexity. The emphasis is on written communication, with a chapter on usage and a glossary. The many samples can be located through the index or table of contents. Indexed.

501. Bowman, Joel P., and Branchaw, Bernadine P. *Business Communication: From Process to Product*. Chicago: Dryden Press, 1987. 663p.

The authors employ a humanistic, problem-solving plan towards increasing the effectiveness of letters, memos, reports, presentations and group work. The communication process is pointed up with exercises, problems and case studies. Model documents appear as textual figures. Indexed.

502. Brill, Laura. *Business Writing Quick and Easy*. New York: AMACOM, 1981. 177p.

Writing hints and suggestions are combined with examples of specific kinds of business writing in this overview. Samples of minutes and meeting summaries appear in chapter nine and examples of procedure manuals in chapter thirteen. The appendices on usage, punctuation, capitalization and related matters form a useful handbook. Not indexed.

503. Brown, Leland. *Communicating Facts and Ideas in Business*. 3d ed. Englewood Cliffs, NJ: Prentice-Hall, 1982. 507p.

Communication principles and the development of general writing skills are considered. The textbook studies planning and problem-solving in letters, reports, oral reports, interviews and presentations. There are some examples but no sample documents. Indexed.

504. Burtness, Paul S., and Hulbert, Jack E. *Effective Business Communication*. 8th ed. Cincinnati, OH: South-Western Publishing Compnay, 1985. 613p.

Elements of writing style are introduced and instructions are supplied for improving letters, memos, reports and oral messages. Samples of shorter written forms can be found through the index. The reference section answers questions on grammar, punctuation and usage. Indexed.

505. Davis, Ken. *Better Business Writing: A Process Approach*. Columbus, OH: Charles E. Merrill, 1983. 208p.

The process approach to business writing used in this volume involves six stages that are useful in any situation. It has been designed to function as a text for writing courses or independent study rather than as a how-to book. Writing rather than business is emphasized, although the organizing and drafting stages for letters and reports are covered. Indexed.

506. DeVries, Mary A. *Guide to Better Business Writing*. Piscataway, NJ: New Century Publishers, 1981. 201p.

Four steps to business writing are presented in this guide and applied to the writing of memos, letters and reports. The roles of style, usage and punctuation in business writing are disclosed. Indexed.

507. DiGaetani, John L.; DiGaetani, Jane B.; and Harbert, Earl N. *Writing Out Loud: A Self-Help Guide to Clear Business Writing*. Homewood, IL: Dow Jones-Irwin, 1983. 178p.

The authors have devised a participative method to writing that stresses conversational text with examples. The brief reference section assists with punctuation, grammar and spelling problems. Indexed.

508. Eisenberg, Anne. *Writing Well for the Technical Professions*. New York: Harper and Row, 1988. 576p.

Volume unavailable for examination.

509. Feinberg, Lilian O. *Applied Business Communication*. Assisted by Mary C. Thompson. Sherman Oaks, CA: Alfred Publishing Company, 1982. 585p.

This is a basic textbook for the workplace. Written skills are the focus of skill development exercises and examples. In the applications section, instruction embraces different types of letters, reports, proposals, memos, meetings, and telephone skills. Punctuation, grammar, spelling and mechanics problems are handled in a separate handbook. Indexed.

510. Feinberg, Susan. *Components of Technical Writing*. New York: Holt, Rinehart and Winston, 1989. 539p.

Volume unavailable for examination.

511. Fielden, John S.; Fielden, Jean D.; and Dulek, Ronald E. *The Business Writing Style Book*. Englewood Cliffs, NJ: Prentice-Hall, 1984. 159p.

For professionals, the book distinguishes different styles of business writing as they relate to particular situations or kinds of writing. Although it is concerned more with writing than with specific applications, some chapters provide how-to information in the form of suggestions and guidelines. Indexed.

512. Figgins, Ross; Golen, Steven P.; and Pearce, C. Glenn. *Business Communication Basics: Applications and Technology*. New York: John Wiley and Sons, 1984. 500p.

The textbook concerns development of effective oral and written communication skills through better letters, reports and other correspondence, listening and presentations. Models appear in the text as illustrations. Unit four shows the impact and use of word processing. A glossary and discussion of the elements of grammar are in the appendices. Indexed.

513. Flower, Linda. *Problem-Solving Strategies for Writing*. 2d ed. San Diego, CA: Harcourt Brace Jovanovich, 1985. 256p.

Using a problem-solving approach, guidelines and strategies are unveiled for planning, organizing, designing and editing documents written for the professional or academic worlds. The book is intended primarily for professionals writing memos and reports. Chapters five through seven and nine through twelve advance nine key steps in the writing process, with examples and exercises. Relevant case studies can be found in chapters three and thirteen. Indexed.

514. Forman, Janis. *The Random House Guide to Business Writing*. With Kathleen A. Kelly. New York: Random House, 1988. 518p.

Volume unavailable for examination.

515. Frank, Darlene. *Silicon English. Business Writing Tools for the Computer Age*. San Rafael, CA: Royall Press, 1985. 212p.

This is a combination of effective writing techniques and basic information on computer usage. Chapter six has brief descriptions of types of writing such as letters, proposals and reports. Editing functions and ghostwriting for the boss are included. A glossary of terms appears in the appendices and a quick-reference guide card in a book pocket. Indexed.

516. Fruehling, Rosemary T., and Oldham, N. B. *Write to the Point! Letters, Memos, and Reports That Get Results*. New York: McGraw-Hill, 1988. 261p.

Style, punctuation and grammar form the basics of good writing. These basics are applied both to writing at work (letters, memos and reports) and writing at home (letters and resumes). The author's plan employs numerous examples of both good and bad writing, but no model documents. Indexed.

517. Harkins, Craig, and Plung, Daniel L., eds. *A Guide for Writing Better Technical Papers*. New York: Institute of Electrical and Electronics Engineers, 1981. 219p.

The forty-eight readings in this compilation were published between 1954 and 1980. The essays and articles investigate techniques, guidelines and suggestions for the improvement of such written documents as reports and presentations. This book is most useful when it accompanys a practical, how-to manual. Indexed.

518. Harty, Kevin J. *Strategies for Business and Technical Writing.* 2d ed. San Diego, CA: Harcourt Brace Jovanovich, 1985. 287p.

The anthology of twenty-eight brief essays studies the writing process and specific documents such as letters, reports and proposals. Some essays have models as examples. There is an extensive annotated bibliography of books, anthologies and journal articles. This collection of reprinted or condensed essays is useful as a supplemnt to a text or a handbook of current practice. Not indexed.

519. Hatch, Richard. *Business Communication: Theory and Technique.* Chicago: Science Research Associates, 1983. 522p.

This business communication textbook is based on the psychological principles of communication. It integrates theory, principles and practice. Adapted from an earlier book, two continuing case studies are used for writing practice. Applications presented are: different kinds of letters, memos, reports and oral presentations. Sample documents are indicated in the index. Indexed.

520. Hatch, Richard. *Business Writing.* Chicago: Science Research Associates, 1983. 474p.

Basically the same as *Business Communication: Theory and Technique*, this version does not have the four chapters on perception, images, symbols and their relationship to communication. Indexed.

521. Hatch, Richard A., and Myers, Robert J. *Business Communication: Principles and Practices.* 2d ed. Chicago: Science Research Associates, 1989. 000p. (Pagination unavailable)

Volume unavailable for examination.

522. Himstreet, William C., and Baty, Wayne M. *A Guide to Business Communication.* Homewood, IL: Learning Systems Company, 1981. 200p.

General writing principles are communicated and then related to letter and report writing. The self-help method has four examinations with answers. The test briefly considers listening and presentations, with pertinent examples and a glossary. Indexed.

523. Hirschhorn, Howard H. *Writing for Science, Industry, and Technology.* New York: Van Nostrand, 1980. 265p.

Critical reading and sources of information are presented. After describing the elements of writing, the book provides practical guidelines for creating letters, manuals, reports, abstracts and oral presentations. It discusses the use of checklists. Indexed.

524. Hudson, Randolph H.; McGuire, Gertrude M.; and Selzler, Bernard J. *Business Writing: Concepts and Applications.* San Diego, CA: Roxbury Publishing Company, 1983. 334p.

A compilation of forty articles on effective communication principles, the business formats investigated are letters, memos and reports. The articles are grouped by topic with questions and cases. There is a model formal report. The appendices include separate glossaries of usage and updated expressions. Indexed.

525. Jones, Barbara S. *Written Communication for Today's Manager.* New York: Lebhar-Friedman Boks, 1980. 160p.

The basics of written communication principles and practices for managers are reviewed. Based on the author's experience and research with retail stores, it furnishes how-to information, a few don'ts and examples. Questions, exercises and cases for each chapter appear in the appendix. This is best used in conjunction with books stressing applications. Not indexed.

526. Kohut, Gary F., and Baxter, Carol M. *Business Communication: A Functional Perspective.* Columbus, OH: Merrill Publishing Company, 1987. 473p.

This process approach to business communication principles and practice emphasizes the development of written communication skills. A basic textbook, letters, memos, short and formal reports, resumes, meetings and presentations are examined. Samples of written documents appear as figures in the text. A guide to grammar and usage is in the appendix. Indexed.

527. Lamphear, Lynn. *Shortcuts to Effective On-the-Job Writing.* Englewood Cliffs, NJ: Prentice-Hall, 1982. 179p.

Advice is offered on improving general writing skills through short cuts and practical techniques. The text has many examples and exercises. Indexed.

528. Lay, Mary K. *Strategies for Technical Writing: A Rhetoric with Readings.* New York: Holt, Rinehart and Winston, 1982. 308p.

The author discusses how to organize material according to basic rhetorical patterns. Students are encouraged to use their freshmen composition skills in their professional writing. The specific applications involved are letters, memos and reports. Writing and organizing are stressed rather than specific formats. Indexed.

529. Locker, Kitty O., and Weeks, Francis W. *Business Writing Cases and Problems.* 1984 ed. Champaign, IL: Stipes Publishing Company, 1984. 200p.

Cases and problems are given for practice in business writing and speaking. The cases are to be used in conjunction with another textbook. The volume contains introductory discussion, outlines and examples. Not indexed.

530. Lord, William J. Jr., and Dawe, Jessamon. *Functional Business Communication.* 3d ed. Englewood Cliffs, NJ: Prentice-Hall, 1983. 611p.

This textbook focuses on problem-solving techniques and writing competencies. Letters and reports are considered with comprehensive coverage of the different kinds of reports. Models appear in the text as figures. Aspects of research such as sampling form part of the discussion. Indexed.

531. McKellen, J. S. *New Business Matters: Practice Materials for Business Communication in English.* Oxford, New York: Pergamon Institute of English, 1985. 168p.

Volume unavailable for examination.

532. Mansfield, Carmella E., and Bahniuk, Margaret H. *Writing Business Letters and Reports.* 2d ed. Mission Hills, CA: Glencoe Publishing Company, Bobbs-Merrill, 1987. 607p.

The authors introduce writing principles and mechanics. These are applied to the writing of letters, memos and different types of reports. Oral communication and the employment process are covered in separate sections. Models appear in the text, with a partial formal report in the appendices. Punctuation, research and special readings are located also in the appendices. Indexed.

533. Mascolini, Marcia V., and Freeman, Caryl P. *Objective Writing for Business and Industry.* Reston, VA: Reston Publishing Company, 1984. 545p.

Case studies and checklists accompany the discussion of the principles and techniques of factual (or objective) writing. Models are given for letters, resumes, abstracts and reports. Grammar and punctuation fundamentals are covered in the appendix. Indexed.

534. Mullins, Carolyn J. *The Complete Writing Guide to Preparing Reports, Proposals, Memos, etc.* Englewood Cliffs, NJ: Prentice-Hall, 1980. 282p.

This specific approach to writing involves scheduling, organizing, standardizing information, rewriting and revising. The method is applied to different kinds of writing only in general terms. The appendix has sample pages for a style sheet. Indexed.

535. Naczi, Frances D. *Without Bombast and Blunders: An Executive's Guide to Effective Writing.* Rockville Centre, NY: Farnsworth Publishing Company, 1980. 178p.

General concepts and simple techniques for improving writing ability are supplied. The techniques identified are used in writing letters, memos and short reports. The book concentrates on style and usage. The author offers suggestions, practical guidelines and some examples. Indexed.

536. Overman, Dean L. *Effective Writing Techniques.* New York: Monarch Press, 1980. 136p.

The author's writing techniques emphasize the development of organizational and structural skills in the use of written language. Sentences and paragraphs for professionals are considered. There is a glossary in chapter eleven. Indexed.

537. Pearce, C. Glenn; Figgins, Ross; and Golen, Steven P. *Principles of Business Communication: Theory, Application, and Technology.* New York: John Wiley and Sons, 1984. 648p.

A basic business communication textbook, practical considerations are stressed in preparing letters, memos, proposals, reports and oral presentations. One unit examines word processing options and equipment. Chapters have models as textual figures. The authors have included a glossary of language and business terms, and a section on grammar and usage (Appendix A). Indexed.

538. Quattrini, Joseph A. *Clear and Simple Technical Writing.* New York: Prentice-Hall, 1986. 170p.

Brief guidelines are advanced for developing clear effective writing. The design checklist (chapter two) requires planning, analyzing, revising and evaluating writing. Limited to written communication, chapter three reviews five problems with models of an abstract and a proposal. Chapter four answers eight problems but without models. Not indexed.

539. Ricks, Betty R., and Gow, Kay F. *Business Communication: Systems and Applications.* New York: John Wiley and Sons, 1987. 479p.

The comprehensive textbook points out the competencies needed for letters, memos, proposals, reports, listening, presentations and resumes. Models are furnished of letters, memos, proposals, resumes and reports. Good guidelines for composing messages for electronic and oral communications are mentioned. Indexed.

540. Riney, Larry A. *Technical Writing for Industry: An Operations Manual for the Technical Writer.* Englewood Cliffs, NJ: Prentice-Hall, 1989. 256p.

Volume unavailable for examination.

541. Rooney, Pamela S., and Supnick, Roberta M. *Business and Professional Writing: A Problem-Solving Approach.* Englewood Cliffs, NJ: Prentice-Hall, 1985. 189p.

A problem-solving approach to writing is disclosed with fourteen cases, exercises and sample memos, letters, proposals and reports. Good writing is seen as the key to success. Grammar and mechanics problems are handled in the appendices. Indexed.

542. Samuels, Marilyn S. *The Technical Writing Process.* New York: Oxford University Press, 1988. 000p. (Pagination unavailable)

Volume unavailable for examination.

543. Sitzmann, Marion. *Successful Business Writing: A Practical Guide for the Student and Professional.* Skokie, IL: National Textbook, 1983. 80p.

Volume unavailable for examination.

544. Stultz, Russell A. *The Business Side of Writing.* Englewood Cliffs, NJ: Prentice-Hall, 1984. 191p.

Written for technical writers, chapters three through five present guidelines for organizing, researching projects, and estimating costs for a projects' completion. Planning and organizing are emphasized rather than writing. Indexed.

545. Sundin, Hakan. *Efficient Communication Presents: More Effective Reports, Memos, and Speeches*. Translated by Janice Young. New York: Vantage Press, 1986. 130p.

A short introduction is provided to planning and presenting oral and written material. Advice and hints are supplied with illustrations and a few examples. Translated from the Swedish, it uses the example of a technical report in discussing the presentation of written work. Not indexed.

546. Tibbetts, Arn; Tibbetts, Charlene; and Steele, Louise. *Practical Business Writing*. Boston: Little, Brown and Company, 1987. 508p.

This textbook is concerned with increasing student ability to write and speak effectively. Help is provided for letters, proposals, reports, resumes and presentations. There are examples of the shorter forms, as indicated in the index. The appendices include a short handbook of grammar and punctuation. Indexed.

547. Tichy, H. J. *Effective Writing for Engineers, Managers, Scientists*. 2d ed. With Sylvia Fourdrinier. New York: John Wiley and Sons, 1988. 580p.

Writing skills, grammar and style are investigated for business and technology writers. Instruction and advice support learning about memos, letters, minutes, reports, and resumes. The book contains no sample documents and few examples. The guide to problem words and phrases in the appendix is arranged alphabetically and could serve as a glossary or dictionary. Indexed.

548. Wolf, Morris P., and Kuiper, Shirley. *Effective Communication in Business*. 9th ed. Cincinnati, OH: South-Western Publishing, 1989. 638p.

Developing skills and awareness is the focus here. The business communication textbook places more emphasis on theory than on practical applications. Letters, memos, reports, and resumes are shown with sample documents. The appendices offer assistance with words, punctuation, letter formats and misspelled words. Indexed.

549. Woolcott, L. A., and Unwin, W. R. *Mastering Business Communication*. London: Macmillan Press, 1983. 309p.

This British business communication textbook takes into account British examination requirements. Specific applications included are correspondence, reports, summaries, manuals, instructions, meetings, listening and speaking. The elements of each form are examined with guidelines, examples, exercises and answers (in the appendices). Later chapters discuss communication theories and methods. A glossary of meeting terms and discussion of grammar and examination techniques are in the appendices. Indexed.

550. Woolston, Donald C.; Robinson, Patricia A.; and Kutzbach, Gisela. *Effective Writing Strategies for Engineers and Scientists*. Chelsea, MI: Lewis Publishers, 1988. 181p.

The authors briefly describe writing techniques and strategies for engineers and scientists. An analytical approach is suggested for those in industry, government and consulting who write at work. There are guidelines and sample outlines for the report and feasibility study sections. The utilization of word processing is encouraged. Common errors, abbreviations and style manuals have been added to the appendices. Indexed.

WRITING SYSTEMS

551. Bjelland, Harley. *Technical Writing -- The Easy Way*. Sparks, NV: Norway Books, 1981. 107p.

Writing techniques for effective letters, memos and reports are supported by guidelines, examples and blank forms. The table of contents effectively outlines the book. One section comments on the use of the call report for telephone messages. A technique delineated, the gazinta, shows the parts of a document pictorially. Indexed.

552. Fielden, John S., and Dulek, Ronald E. *Bottom-line Business Writing*. Englewood Cliffs, NJ: Prentice-Hall, 1984. 156p.

The book contains thirteen rules for writing more direct and organized documents. The specific method, bottom-line writing, is presented with examples of specific kinds of writing scattered in the text. The book has to be read in its entirety in order to understand the method completely. Indexed.

553. Harty, Kevin J., and Keenan, John. *Writing for Business and Industry: Process and Product*. New York: Macmillan, 1987. 354p.

The PAFEO method has five steps: purpose, audience, format, evidence, and organization. The writing of letters, proposals, summaries, abstracts and reports is demonstrated, with examples and a sample formal report. Word usage, grammar, punctuation and spelling problems are in part five. The appendix covers word processing. Indexed.

554. Keenan, John. *Feel Free to Write. A Guide for Business and Professional People*. New York: John Wiley and Sons, 1982. 190p.

This general introduction to writing skills for managers and professionals uses the PAFEO method. Letters, memos and reports are discussed in part five, with samples only of letters. There are self-teaching projects in each chapter. Some coverage of usage and grammar is also provided along with useful references to other sources. Indexed.

555. Markel, Michael H., and Lucier, R. J. *Make Your Point. A Guide to Improving Your Business and Technical Writing*. Englewood Cliffs, NJ: Prentice-Hall, 1983. 136p.

In this writing system, the structure reflects the purpose. Writing principles are combined with guidelines and checklists for letters, memos and reports. Samples for revision can be found in the appendix. There is a selected handbook on punctuation, style and mechanics. Indexed.

556. Morris, John O. *Make Yourself Clear!* New York: McGraw-Hill, 1980. 236p.

The author's system, behind the words, aims at improving oral and written communications. A series of basic principles are supplemented with cases and problems as examples. This first paperback edition includes a checklist of questions (at the end of the book) for editing written documents. Indexed.

557. Sandra Pakin and Associates. *Documentation Development Methodology: Techniques for Improved Communications*. Englewood Cliffs, NJ: Prentice-Hall, 1984. 231p.

The DDM (document development methodology) method produces clear technical documents. There are checklists and examples for the planning, writing and producing stages. A sample project plan and a project-writing guide appear in the appendices. A glossary has been provided. Indexed.

558. Stockard, Olivia, and Margolis, Frederic. *The Complete Business Writing Kit: All the Skills You Need in 10 Self Instructional Lessons*. New York: John Wiley and Sons, 1989. 238p.

Volume unavailable for examination.

559. Weiss, Edmond H. *The Writing System for Engineers and Scientists*. Englewood Cliffs, NJ: Prentice-Hall, 1982. 274p.

Writing strategies and editing highlight this writing system. The system is the result of six years of work with seminars. There are guidelines and checklists for planning, designing, drafting and producing proposals, reports and other documents. Indexed.

560. Westheimer, Patricia H., and Senteney, Jacqueline S. *The Executive Style Book*. Glenview, IL: Scott Foresman, 1988. 224p.

The authors have developed a five step process for writing called the speakwrite method. The five steps (speak, plan, format, write, and rewrite) are used in writing letters and memos (with samples). Early chapters discuss the guidelines and rules for writing with style. A chapter is devoted to the use of word processing and the appendix addresses problems with words, usage and misspellings. Indexed.

Chapter 5

WRITTEN COMMUNICATION

Numerous articles decry the quality of writing now being done by students, managers and engineers. When individuals are unable to communicate their ideas in printed documents, all areas of the workplace are affected. The business plan required to acquire venture capital fails or product instructions generate complaints rather than sales. Excellent written documents bring success in both the business and technical fields.

This chapter lists books with guidelines, proven techniques and sample documents for improved written products. There are four major areas: general correspondence, company-oriented publications, career development materials, and specialty documents. Most of the paper generated in a work environment takes the form of letters and memos. Numerous published books advance well-tested approaches to memo and letter writing, and display many examples. In business, effective written communication is synonymous with mastery of these skills.

The process of beginning, developing and maintaining a business necessitates business plans, marketing plans, annual reports and catalogs. For the novice and those needing improvement, there are tips, outlines and samples of finished products of such documents. Internal communication, other than correspondence, takes the form of company-sponsored publications, employee publications and newsletters. Each has a unique format and specific requirements. In some works listed here, experts disclose how-to instructions, advice and strategies.

The pursuit of the perfect job and correct career choice requires another written product, the resume. Previously directed at beginners in the job market, many newly-published works consider mid-career changes and advancement within and outside the organization. The different types of resumes are shown as one step towards career development and career change.

The largest section of Chapter 5 concerns the specialized document; i.e., instructions, manuals, proposals, abstracts, summaries, and reports. Each of these document types requires special attention to purpose, audience and content. Practitioners and teachers reveal solutions for each problem that has to be handled.

ABSTRACTS

561. Barnes, Gregory A. *Write for Success: A Guide for Business and the Professions*. Philadelphia: ISI Press, 1986. 154p.

As part of the ISIS Professional Writing Series, the business writer is guided through the principles of writing, rewriting, editing and publishing. Chapter twelve on abstracts and summaries and the Quick Guide to Punctuation are especially useful. This is not a how-to book. There is a bibliography of the sources used and an index to help the reader. Indexed.

562. Cremmins, Edward T. *The Art of Abstracting*. Philadelphia: ISI Press, 1982. 150p.

The author advances both rules and practice for three kinds of reading: retrieval, creative and critical. The reading methods presented are employed in writing abstracts. Although advice is given, with examples and exercises, the text concentrates on reading and thinking skills. Appendix two lists the reading rules needed for abstracting. There is a glossary. Indexed.

563. Eisenberg, Anne. *Effective Technical Communication*. New York: McGraw-Hill, 1982. 355p.

After an introduction to basic technical writing, this textbook focuses on practice in creating abstracts, proposals, reports, letters and oral presentations. Examples, suggestions and exercises are provided. The models can be located through the index or table of contents. Appendix B covers grammar and usage trouble spots. Indexed.

564. Markel, Michael H. *Technical Writing: Situations and Strategies*. New York: St. Martin's Press, 1984. 538p.

The author debates the process and techniques of technical writing. The techniques are applied to the writing of abstracts, letters, different types of reports and oral presentations. Memos are considered as memo reports. Chapters include a useful writer's checklist and examples. Indexed.

565. Timm, Paul R., and Jones, Christopher G. *Business Communication. Getting Results*. 2d ed. Englewood Cliffs, NJ: Prentice-Hall, 1987. 509p.

The functional aspects of writing are highlighted. The mechanics of the English language are consideered in relation to letters, reports, presentations, abstracts and resumes. Samples of the shorter written forms can be found through the table of contents. A brief guide to usage and punctuation is in the appendix. Indexed.

ANNUAL REPORTS

566. Grinling, Jasper. *The Annual Report. A Guide to Planning, Producing and Promoting Company Reports*. Aldershot, Hants, England, UK: Gower Publishing Company, 1986. 137p.

This is a guide to the design, preparation, distribution and marketing of annual reports for companies in England. The principles presented are applicable anywhere. The company report planner, which accompanies the book, has a chronological planning chart with four categories: design, distribution, shareholders, and the employee report. There are few examples. Indexed.

567. Winter, Elmer L. *A Complete Guide to Preparing a Corporate Annual Report.* New York: Van Nostrand Reinhold, 1985. 414p.

The content of an annual report is analyzed. Strategies for creating a better presentation appear with the basic elements of the report. There are sample forms and model letters to shareholders. Indexed.

BUSINESS PLANS

568. Bradway, Bruce M., and Pritchard, Robert E. *Developing the Business Plan for a Small Business.* New York: AMACOM, 1980. 50p.

The authors show how to write a business plan and why it should be done. While focusing on a five-year plan, the book also describes finance, marketing, advertising and promotion for the small business. A detailed outline of a business plan appears as exhibit one. There are examples of the financial statements. Not indexed.

569. Brooks, Julie K., and Stevens, Barry A. *How to Write a Successful Business Plan.* New York: AMACOM, 1987. 231p.

The process of writing a business plan is followed from idea to final presentation. Managers and owners can use this process (as outlined in appendix A) and the sample plan (appendix B) in planning for growth and/or specific objectives. The reading list by topic identifies useful related works. Indexed.

570. Burton, E. James, and McBride, W. Blan. *Total Business Planning: A Step-by-Step Guide With Forms.* New York: John Wiley and Sons, 1988. 205p.

Volume unavailable for examination.

571. *Business Planning Guide.* Dover, NH: Upstart Publishing Company, 1985. 122p.

This brief guide to designing and writing a business plan is arranged in the order recommended for the plan. Sections of the book contain practical advice and examples from a real business plan. The appendices provide a sample partnership agreement, glossary and blank worksheets. Not indexed.

572. Butler, Robert E., and Rappaport, Donald. *Money and Your Business. I. How to Get It. Guide 1 The Business Plan -- A Basic Tool.* Edited by Alan M. Disman. New York: New York Institute of Finance, 1982. 132p.

Part of a three volume series, guide one considers the development of a business plan. Many charts and figures accompany the written description. The index for each section allows the entrepreneur to refer to the appropriate part. Each guide has a detailed table of contents and list of exhibits. Indexed.

573. Delaney, Robert V. Jr., and Howell, Robert A. *How to Prepare an Effective Business Plan. A Step-by-Step Guide.* New York: AMACOM, 1986. 271p.

A self-study guide for managers on developing business plans, the volume proceeds step-by-step. The book has an outline, sample plan and blank worksheets. Part five consists of five readings. There is a method for analyzing and planning product lines in the appendix. Not indexed.

574. Hosmer, LaRue, and Guiles, Roger. *Creating the Successful Business Plan for New Ventures*. New York: McGraw-Hill, 1985. 213p.

While emphasizing the planning process needed to create or expand a business, the book investigates the busines plan and its presentation. There is a model plan in appendix A. Indexed.

575. Kravitt, Gregory I. *How To Raise Capital. Preparing and Presenting a Business Plan*. Homewood, IL: Dow Jones-Irwin, 1984. 187p.

Entreprenuers are guided through raising venture capital and writing a business plan. Organized like a workbook, a question and answer format is employed. Two sample business plans are in part two. Indexed.

576. Luther, William M. *How to Develop a Business Plan in 15 Days*. New York: AMACOM, 1987. 241p.

The title is misleading as this book promotes an approach to corporate planning that stresses the cooperative development of a business plan. The project requires fifteen days and involves the work of many different individuals within a company. An illustration of a hypothetical business plan outline is shown. Indexed.

577. McKeever, Mike P. *Start-Up Money. How to Create a Business Plan and Loan Package to Finance Your Small Business*. 2d ed. Berkeley, CA: Nolo Press, 1986. 194p.

Instructions on preparing a business plan and loan package are revealed. This volume emphasizes starting and financing a small business, with detailed forms and illustrations. Sample business plans and blank forms are in the appendices. Not indexed.

578. McLaughlin, Harold J. *Building Your Business Plan. A Step-by-Step Approach*. New York: John Wiley and Sons, 1985. 297p.

A business plan is developed one part at a time using examples and a case study. The appendices to chapters two and seven show two successful plans as presented to the investment community. Indexed.

579. Mancuso, Joseph R. *How to Prepare and Present a Business Plan*. Englewood Cliffs, NJ: Prentice-Hall, 1983. 316p.

The author uses a workbook method to write a business plan and prepare the case for raising venture capital. The text offers advice on planning and tailoring the plan to the company. The appendices include a questionnaire, checklist, glossary, three full-length business plans and five outlined plans. Indexed.

580. Mancuso, Joseph R. *How to Write a Winning Business Plan*. Englewood Cliffs, NJ: Prentice-Hall, 1985. 344p.

Step-by-step procedures and guidelines are shown for creating a successful business plan. Portions of this work appeared in the author's 1983 book, *How to Prepare and Present a Business Plan*. The appendices contain a checklist, questionnaire, outline, glossary and sample business plans. Indexed.

581. Oppenheimer, Matt, and Young, Gerry A. *Computer-Assisted Business Plans*. Englewood Cliffs, NJ: Prentice-Hall, 1986. 287p.

This is a tutorial for the preparation of business plans and reports using a computer. Samples of parts of a business plan and several computer plans appear in the Aappendix. There is a basic glossary. The tutorial can be used with or without a computer. Indexed.

582. Osgood, William R. *How to Plan and Finance Your Business*. Boston: CBI Publishing Company, 1980. 165p.

The author presents guidelines and a suggested outline for preparing a business plan. The text has a sample business plan, glossary and worksheets. Not indexed.

583. Osgood, William R.; Fletcher, William; and Curtin, Dennis P. *Preparing Your Business Plan with Excel*. Berkeley, CA: Osborne McGraw-Hill, 1986. 412p.

Business plan guidelines from the author's earlier book are combined with instructions for Microsoft Excel. Key elements, checklists and the contents of a business plan are displayed with careful notes on use of the software. There is a disk available that accompanys the text version. Indexed.

584. Osgood, William R., and Curtin, Dennis P. *Preparing Your Business Plan with Lotus 1-2-3*. Englewood Cliffs, NJ: Prentice-Hall; Somerville, MA: Curtin and London, 1984. 170p.

The authors suggest a format and model outline for a business plan using Lotus 1-2-3 and a microcomputer. Software tips are in the table of contents and blank worksheets are in the back of the book. A computer disk to accompany the text is available. Indexed.

585. Osgood, William R., and Curtin, Dennis P. *Preparing Your Business Plan with Multiplan*. Somerville, MA: Curtin and London; Englewood Cliffs, NJ: Prentice-Hall, 1985. 154p.

Like the other works by this author, the book contains samples of the business plan and practical steps for using Multiplan. The table of contents has tips for the business plan and for the use of Multiplan. Indexed.

586. Osgood, William R., and Curtin, Dennis P. *Preparing Your Business Plan with Symphony*. Somerville, MA: Curtin and London: Englewood Cliffs, NJ: Prentice-Hall, 1985. 218p.

A complete business plan is prepared with Symphony. Using the same arrangement as the other books in the series, there are tips on the plan and on the software. The text has a sample plan, worksheets and an accompanying disk. Indexed.

587. Osgood, William R., and Maupin, J. David. *Preparing Your Business Plan: Multiplan on the DEC Rainbow*. Burlington, MA: Digital Press, 1985. 153p.

The author's well-developed guidelines on the business plan are joined to directions on Multiplan with a DEC Rainbow. There are separate tip sections for the plan, the software and the equipment. Indexed.

588. Rich, Stanley R., and Gumpert, David E. *Business Plans That Win $$$*. New York: Harper and Row, 1985. 220p.

Developed from the MIT Enterprise Forum evening sessions, preparation of a business plan is presented as part of a process aimed at achieving corporate excellence and profitability. The plan appears in chapter two. The index should be used to locate the key elements of a business plan. There is a directory of forum locations. Indexed.

589. Siegel, Eric S.; Schultz, Loren A.; and Ford, Brian R. *The Arthur Young Business Plan Guide*. Edited by David C. Carney. New York: John Wiley and Sons, 1987. 184p.

The authors recommend steps for planning and preparing a business plan. After an introduction, a model plan from Good Foods Inc. is dissected with explanation. Indexed.

590. Taylor, James W. *How to Create a Winning Business Plan*. New York: Alexander Hamilton Institute, 1986. 239p.

Volume unavailable for examination.

591. Welsh, John A., and White, Jerry F. *The Entrepreneur's Master Planning Guide*. Englewood Cliffs, NJ: Prentice-Hall, 1983. 408p.

The process of launching a successful business is revealed. Part one offers the elements of a business plan. There are three sample business plans in the appendices. Indexed.

592. West, Alan. *A Business Plan: Planning for the Small Business*. New York: Nichols Publishing Company, 1988. 196p.

The business plan is approached as part of the planning process for a small business. There are guidelines, case studies and examples. Indexed.

593. Williams, Edward E., and Manzo, Salvatore E. *Business Planning for the Entrepreneur: How to Write and Execute a Business Plan*. New York: Van Nostrand Reinhold, 1983. 200p.

The authors focus on the planning and mechanics involved in the business plan. Examination of the book reveals the outline and structure of the plan. There are three sample plans. Indexed.

594. *You and Your Business Plan: A Serious Guide for Serious Entrepreneurs*. Kawkawlin: MI: Webster and Associates, 1986. 33p.

This brief guide is designed for entrepreneurs in new start-up businesses. Divided into thirteen key segments, over one hundred specific guidelines are given for business plan preparation. Each section describes its function and the approaches and/or choices available. The table of contents is an outline of a business plan. Not indexed.

CATALOGS

595. *How to Create Successful Catalogs.* Colorado Springs, CO: Maxwell Sroge Publishing, 1985. 459p.

Techniques are advanced for creating a successful mail order catalog. The volume delineates tasks, required steps, checklists and examples of pages and forms. There is an outline of the thirty eight steps in production and a useful glossary. Indexed.

COMPANY PUBLICATIONS

596. *Human Resource Management. Personnel Practices/Communications.* Chicago: Commerce Clearing House, 1988. One volume looseleaf.

This volume, part of a five volume looseleaf service on human resource management, discloses personnel matters from training and work rules through benefits. One section is concerned with modes of communication. Suggestions are offered for meetings, interviews, bulletin boards, handbooks and newsletters. There are examples and sample newsletter stories. Indexed.

597. Level, Dale A., Jr., and Galle, William P., Jr. *Managerial Communication.* Plano, TX: Business Publications, 1988. 441p.

This organizational communication textbook has the requisite questions, cases and exercises. Section three on sending and receiving messages analyzes listening, interviewing, oral reports and written company publications (policies, procedures, handbooks and manuals). There are guidelines and examples, with sample forms for the interviews. Indexed.

598. Maddalena, Lucille A. *A Communications Manual for Nonprofit Organizations.* New York: AMACOM, 1981. 222p.

The manual relates procedures for setting up a communications program for non-profit organizations. It briefly elaborates on press releases, announcements, fundraising annual reports, and newsletters. There is a glossary and some sample forms. Indexed.

EMPLOYEE PUBLICATIONS

599. Anson, Edward M. III. *How to Prepare and Write Your Employee Handbook.* New York: American Management Associations Publications Group, 1984. 221p.

This workbook consists of a sample employee handbook. The instructional information pages, which are in blue, explain the reason for each policy. Employers can use the workbook to create detailed, written personnel policies. Sample policies appear in the appendices. Indexed.

600. Harris, Joan. *Create Your Employee Handbook -- Fast and Professionally.* Westbury, NY: Asher-Gallant Press, 1984. 82p.

The concise guide to creating an employee handbook has model forms and a sample handbook. Part four supplies reproducible handbook pages for the draft and final print versions. Not indexed.

601. Newsom, Doug, and Siegfried, Tom. *Writing in Public Relations Practice: Form and Style.* Belmont, CA: Wadsworth Publishing Company, 1981. 364p.

While basically an introduction to public relations writing, part four investigates annual reports, employee publications, newsletters, memos, letters and reports. No models are available, but there are numerous examples. Indexed.

602. *Personnel Management: Communications.* Englewood Cliffs, NJ: Prentice-Hall, 1988. One volume looseleaf.

The looseleaf service is designed as a current blueprint for effective communication. For managers, there are instructions and examples on communicating with employees through letters, memos, employee handbooks, reports, meetings, speeches and interviews. The volume has a checklist for the employee handbook. The report bulletins describe new techniques. Indexed.

603. Williams, Patrick. *The Employee Annual Report: Purpose, Format, and Content.* Chicago: Lawrence Ragan Communications, 1983. 114p.

The author concisely describes how and why to create an employee annual report. The basic elements are given with examples, checklists and profiles from some exmployee annual reports. Not indexed.

FEASIBILITY STUDIES

604. Dumont, Raymond A., and Lannon, John M. *Business Communication.* 2d ed. Glenview,IL: Scott Foresman, 1987. 602p.

Oral and written communication are studied with this textbook. It concentrates on letters, reports, proposals, resumes, listening and presenations. Each chapter has a checklist at the back. The text examines word processing and the use of computers in research and graphics. There are sample documents for resumes, letters, proposals and reports (feasibility, memorandum). The appendix is a review of grammar and usage. Indexed.

605. Kantorowitz, Thelma D., and Ott, Catherine R. *Effective Writing for the Business World.* Boston: Little, Brown and Company, 1984. 360p.

A process approach to writing is combined with problem-solving applications. The book furnishes definitions of terms and samples of letters, formal report, proposals and a feasibility study. Indexed.

606. McNally, Terry, and Schiff, Peter. *Contemporary Business Writing: A Problem-Solving Approach.* Belmont, CA: Wadsworth Publishing Company, 1986. 641p.

This desktop reference employs a process approach to solve writing problems. The applications chapters deal with the letter, formal report, proposals and a feasibility study. There are definitions of terms, examples and samples. Boldface numbers in the index refer to a definition's location. Indexed.

607. Miles, James; Bush, Donald; and Kaplan, Allin. *Technical Writing: Principles and Practice*. Chicago: Science Research Associates, 1982. 305p.

An integrated textbook, the principles and techniques of technical writing are merged with applications. Guidelines and models are disclosed for letters, memos, proposals, progress reports and feasibility studies. A guide to usage appears in the appendices. Indexed.

608. Stuart, Ann. *The Technical Writer*. New York: Holt, Rinehart and Winston, 1988. 339p.

The author first presents the use of word processing and the basics of technical writing, style, and editing. Techniques are applied, with checklists and outlines, to the development of letters, memos, resumes, proposals, feasibility reports, formal reports, presentations, and such working reports as software documentation. There are sample memos, resumes, proposals, feasibility reports and a formal report. Part five is a handbook of grammar and punctuation. Indexed.

INSTRUCTIONS

609. Andrews, Deborah C., and Andrews, William D. *Business Communication*. New York: Macmillan; London: Collier Macmillan, 1988. 623p.

The initial chapters contain business communication principles and concepts. Later chapters of the textbook study specific kinds of communication. Skills involved are revising, word processing skills, letters, memos, proposals, reports, instructions, company publications, interviews, meetings and presentations. The authors offer strategies, guidelines, case studies and models of letters, memos, resumes, instructions and reports. The models appear as figures in the text. There is also a handbook to grammar, punctuation and misused words. Indexed.

610. Hicks, Tyler G., and Valorie, Carl M. Sr. *Handbook of Effective Technical Communication*. New York: McGraw-Hill, 1989. 460p.

The handbook encourages engineers, technical writers and managers to write more effectively by following specific techniques, guidelines and shortcuts. The authors concentrate on the major writing tasks which are reports, proposals, specifications, procedures, instruction manuals, catalogs, letters and resumes. There are many examples, checklists of most documents and samples (letters, resumes and parts of a report). One section briefly reviews the key points of grammar and usage. The unique glossary includes terms used by printers and the publishing industry. Indexed.

611. Kolin, Philip C. *Successful Writing at Work*. 2d ed. Lexington, MA: D. C. Heath, 1986. 555p.

The practical approach emphasizes essential skills for career advancement. The volume debates communication, language and usage and research skills. Letters, memos, instructions, proposals, reports and oral presentations are created with examples and some models, including one of a long report. Indexed.

612. McMurray, David A. *Processes in Technical Writing*. New York: Macmillan; London: Collier Macmillan, 1988. 802p.

This textbook employs a process approach in teaching writing skills. The principles provided are applied to letters, memos, instructions, proposals, resumes and different kinds of reports (progress, feasibility, technical). There are tips and models (as indicated in the index). A handbook of usage and a glossary are in the appendices. Indexed.

613. Niederlander, Carol; Kvernes, David; and Sutherland, Sam. *Practical Writing. A Process Approach to Business and Technical Communication*. New York: Holt, Rinehart and Winston, 1986. 434p.

Practical writing problems are addressed. Problems are defined and responses designed for letters, memos, instructions, abstracts, proposals, reports and oral presentations. One section of the textbook considers information gathering. There are samples of a proposal and a report. The appendices cover style, grammar and mechanics, outlines, definitions and crediting sources. Indexed.

614. Pearsall, Thomas E., and Cunningham, Donald H. *How to Write for the World of Work*. 3d ed. New York: Holt, Rinehart and Winston, 1986. 460p.

This textbook provides guidance in writing correspondence, instructions, proposals and different types of reports. Basic principles are reviewed and applied to specific documents with examples. Part four is a handbook of grammar, punctuation and usage. Indexed.

615. Pickett, Nell A., and Laster, Ann A. *Technical English: Writing, Reading, and Speaking*. 5th ed. New York: Harper and Row, 1988. 757p.

Practice is offered in writing memos, letters and reports. The textbook includes directions, with blank planning sheets and examples or samples, of instructions, summaries, resumes, memos, letters and different kinds of reports (progress, investigative, observations, feasibility, and proposals). Part two is a collection of thirteen related readings reprinted from other sources. Part three is a handbook of grammar, usage and mechanics. The inside back cover has a checklist for revising a paper. Indexed.

616. Quible, Zane K.; Johnson, Margaret H.; and Mott, Dennis L. *Introduction to Business Communication*. 2d ed. Englewood Cliffs, NJ: Prentice-Hall, 1988. 554p.

After discussing the basic communication and writing skills, the textbook concentrates on developing skills for letters, reports, resumes and administrative writing (proposals, manuals, instructions and evaluations). Some guidelines are offered. Sample pages and parts of the various documents illustrate the text. The appendices review grammar, punctuation, letter formats and legal issues. Indexed.

617. Zimmerman, Carolyn M., and Campbell, John J. *Fundamentals of Procedure Writing*. 2d ed. Columbia, MD: GP Publishing, 1988. 228p.

Writing effective procedures with the authors' process approach follows three steps (planning, drafting and reviewing). There are useful techniques and examples in the book. The drafting stage includes format, document design, mechanics, style and usage. Appendix B reveals procedures for validating instructions. There is a separate list of figures and tables. Indexed.

LETTERS

618. Booher, Dianna D. *Letter Perfect: A Handbook of Model Letters for the Busy Executive*. Lexington, MA: Lexington Books, 1988. 524p.

Volume unavailable for examination.

619. Bosticco, Mary. *Instant Business Letters*. 2d ed. Aldershot, Hampshire, UK: Gower Publishing Company, 1985. 173p.

After a general discussion of letter writing, part two considers eleven different kinds of letters. Each chapter, after describing the letter, has sample statements for the opening, body and closing. Models are adaptable to different situations. The sections are constructed to be sorted easily on a word processor and used as needed. The book, which forms a valuable guide to developing an individual letter-writing style, was reprinted in 1988. Not indexed.

620. Bosticco, Mary. *Personal Letters for Business People*. 3d ed. Brookfield, VT: Gower Publishing Company, 1986. 351p.

The ninety courtesy letters can be used to create goodwill or help run a business more smoothly. Some of the letters provided are those of recommendation, introduction, invitation, acceptance, thank you, sympathy, and refusal. Chapters have numerous models. Those having to create specialty letters for the first time will find this volume valuable. Not indexed.

621. Brock, Luther A. *Sales Lead-Getting Model Letter Book*. Englewood Cliffs, NJ: Prentice-Hall, 1986. 261p.

This how-to book contains mostly model letters. There are instructions on how to adapt them to different situations. The eight categories, for sales people and managers, are easily found through the detailed table of contents. Not indexed.

622. Cook, Mary F. *Personnel Manager's Portfolio of Model Letters*. Englewood Cliffs, NJ: Prentice-Hall, 1985. 198p.

For managers, writing letters becomes a snap with this handy guide. It fosters the development of a personal style for the composition of impressive letters in the human resource area. Checklists and tips accompany the many samples. There is a separate letter locater index. Indexed.

623. Cross, Mary. *Persuasive Business Writing: Creating Better Letters, Memos, Reports and More*. New York: AMACOM, 1987. 179p.

Persuasive writing techniques are employed for basic business documents. Strategies from sales and advertising are used to create letters, memos and reports. While not a how-to book, the examples and sample report structure can improve the written product. Indexed.

624. Cypert, Samuel A. *Writing Effective Business Letters, Memos, Proposals, and Reports*. Chicago: Contemporary Books, 1983. 309p.

With this basic self-help book, effective memos, letters, proposals and reports can be produced. A positive approach to problem solving is used. Advice is related with tips, checklists and numerous models. Indexed.

625. Durr, Kenneth I.; Durr, Gloria E.; and White, Ralph L. *A Practical Approach to Writing Business Letters*. 2d ed. Dubuque, IA: Kendall/Hunt Publishing, 1984. 275p.

The concepts and procedures of writing business letters are contained in a textbook or ready reference guide. The table of contents indicates specific kinds of letters and their representative models. For basic letters, the text shows the beginning, middle and the end. Not indexed.

626. Elliott, Stephen P. *The Complete Book of Contemporary Business Letters*. Ridgefield, CT: Round Lake Publishing, 1988. 480p.

Volume unavailable for examination.

627. Fahner, Hal, and Miller, Morris E. *Sales Manager's Model Letter Desk Book*. 2d ed. Englewood Cliffs, NJ: Prentice-Hall, 1988. 299p.

This is a compilation of model letters for sales managers. Grouped by category, the function of each letter is cited with models. These proven letters, which were contributed by sales managers, are designed to improve letter writing and produce results. Chapter eight deals with memorandums. The second edition combines the best letters from the previous edition with over one hundred new ones. Not indexed.

628. Farber, William M. *Business Letters Simplified and Self-Taught*. New York: Arco Publishing, 1983. 154p.

The author combines a style book on writing mechanics with a collection of model letters. Intended to promote a less-formal mode of communication, the many models cover different occasions and formats. There are step-by-step instructions and diagrams. Indexed.

629. Frailey, Lester. *Handbook of Business Letters*. Revised by Susan P. Mamchack and Steven R. Mamchack. 3d ed. Englewood Cliffs, NJ: Prentice-Hall, 1988. 928p.

Volume unavailable for examination.

630. Gartside, L. *Model Business Letters*. 3d ed. Estover, Plymouth, UK: Macdonald and Evans, 1981. 530p.

A collection of six hundred models, the letters are written in a modern English style. They are meant to illustrate the principles of good business writing. There is a separate classified list of letters. Indexed.

631. Geffner, Andrea B. *Business Letters the Easy Way*. Woodbury, NY: Barron's Educational Series, 1983. 168p.

Adapted from the author's book, *How to Write Better Business Letters*, the text introduces style and how to create different types of letters, memos and letter reports. The numerous sample letters which are listed in the table of model letters. There is a brief glossary of business terms. Indexed.

632. Geffner, Andrea B. *How to Write Better Business Letters*. Woodbury, NY: Barron's Educational Series, 1982. 144p.

This brief guide to writing correspondence has practical suggestions, examples, and model letters. Chapters three through thirteen promote the writing of specific letters and other correspondence. There is a table of model letters and a glossary of business terms. Indexed.

633. Geil, Lloyd H. *Executive's Desk Manual of Modern Model Business Letters*. Englewood Cliffs, NJ: Executive Reports Corporation, 1980. 1409p.

A collection of model letters for executives, the guidelines summarize each letters intent and suggest modifications. Letters are grouped by subject with an instant locater index. Chapter thirteen offers letters for the secretary, chapter twelve, good writing practices with checklists. Indexed.

634. Glatthorn, Allan A. *Writing for Success*. Glenview, IL: Scott Foresman, 1985. 134p.

The author briefly looks at writing business letters, particularly those delivering bad news, praising oneself, admitting mistakes and giving directions. The very practical guidelines can be adapted to any memo or letter style. Exercises are included along with examples and a usage checklist entitled Sore Thumb. Indexed.

635. Hakoun, Mitchell and Tomlinson, Gerald. *Accountant's Complete Model Letter Book*. Englewood Cliffs, NJ: Prentice-Hall, 1987. 424p.

A compilation of three hundred models, the letters in this volume were chosen from those submitted by accounting firms. The letters concentrate on general correspondence, personnel management, recommendations, office management and tax related correspondence. Proposals and report writing for accountants are also communicated. A separate handbook covers letter formats. Indexed.

636. Harris, Joan. *Modern Business Letters: 70 Ready-to-Use Models*. Westbury, NY: Asher-Gallant Press, 1985. 88p.

There are seventy model business letters in twelve categories for business executives. The categories include: claims, credit, reply, sales, public relations, personal, and personnel letters. The margin notes aid in revising and personalizing the model letters. Writing tips are provided. Not indexed.

637. Henry, Donald L. and Henry, Fay W. *The Banker's Portfolio of Model Letters*. Englewood Cliffs, NJ: Prentice-Hall, 1988. 566p.

Over four hundred sample letters are grouped in twenty subject areas. A brief discussion of how to write a business letter precedes the collection. Each model letter has an accompanying explanation that details its use. While aimed at bankers and the financial industry, the letters on community activity, human resources and personal situations have a wider application. A cross index, the Locato-matic, to subjects and ideas is provided. The appendices list government agencies, quick reference tools and describe formats. Indexed.

638. Holtz, Herman R. *The Business Writing Problem Solver*. Homewood, IL: Dow Jones-Irwin, 1987. 235p.

Made up almost entirely of models, this book can be used to create letters, proposals, reports and other documents. Explanations, guidelines, and advice are provided for the models. The book focuses on letter content and the development of an individual set of models. Indexed.

639. Keyworth, Cynthia L. *Letters That Get Action*. New York: Arco Publishing, 1984. 184p.

The volume contains advice on putting ideas into letters that work, particularly consumer action and citizen action letters. While only of peripheral interest to business letter writers, the discussion of letter writing basics is good. Indexed.

640. Kight, Leila K. *The Business Researcher's Handbook*. Washington, DC: Washington Researchers, 1980. 153p.

While designed as a handbook for small business or researchers, the book has descriptions and samples of letters, proposals and reports. There are evaluation forms. Not indexed.

641. Kuswa, Webster. *The Sales Rep's Letter Book*. New York: AMACOM, 1984. 216p.

Guidelines and checklists are supplied for writing sales letters and proposals and for improving writing skills. The circumstances and specifics for different types of letters are furnished with model letters. Indexed.

642. Lee, LaJuana W., et al. *Business Communication*. Chicago: Rand McNally, 1980. 467p.

A conversational tone explains the principles, functions and techniques of business communication. The authors combine skill development with practice in creating letters, reports and presentations. The ten appendices disclose abbreviations, usage techniques, word processing guidance and a glossary. Indexed.

643. Lesikar, Raymond V. *Business Communication: Theory and Application*. 5th ed. Homewood, IL: Richard D. Irwin, 1984. 572p.

Communication theory is summarized and applied to writing letters and reports and creating oral presentations. Models of letters and reports are in the text as figures. Formats and checklists are given in the appendices. Indexed.

644. Love, Charles, and Tinervia, Joseph. *Commercial Correspondence for Students of English as a Second Language*. 2d ed. New York: McGraw-Hill, 1980. 197p.

This textbook promotes the writing of business correspondence in English. Grammar and usage are reviewed as well as letters, resumes and memos. It should be valuable for the non-English-proficient business person. Not indexed.

645. McKellen, J. S., and Spooner, M. D. *Business Matters: Practice Materials for Business Communication in English*. Oxford: Pergamon Press, 1982. 101p.

Meant primarily for foreign students, the book sponsors practice in writing effective letters. Discussion, checklists, exercises and examples of the models are provided. Recorded material accompanying the text deals with verbal skills such as telephone conversations and meetings. Teachers notes can be found in the appendix. Not indexed.

646. Meyer, Harold E. *Lifetime Encyclopedia of Letters*. Englewood Cliffs, NJ: Prentice-Hall, 1983. 403p.

The encyclopedia compiles model letters into 533 categories, both business and personal ones. Preceeding each category is a basic outline demonstrating how to write the letter. Indexed.

647. Murphy, Herta A., and Hildebrandt, Herbert W. *Effective Business Communications*. 5th ed. New York: McGraw-Hill, 1988. 730p.

The business communications textbook begins with general skills, particularly those related to letters, memos, proposals, reports, resumes, presentations, listening, speaking and meetings. The text stresses understanding human behavior and designing messages accordingly. There are examples, checklists and models (letters, memos, resumes, proposals and a memo report). The checklists are listed at the end of the table of contents. There are samples pages from formal report. Mechanics and style are handled in the appendix. Indexed.

648. Nauheim, Ferd. *Letter Perfect. How to Write Business Letters that Work*. New York: Van Nostrand Reinhold, 1982. 224p.

The authors highlight the development of mental attitudes that produce strong letters rather than the technical aspects of letter writing. More emphasis is placed on sales and customer letters. The exercises in chapter eighteen suggest replies and analyses. The instant locator has five parts, the most useful of which is the index by purpose. Not indexed.

649. Paxson, William C. *Write It Now!* Reading, MA: Addison-Wesley, 1985. 146p.

Techniques are shown for organizing, outlining, and writing ten documents: a summary, proposals, letters, memos and several kinds of reports. The practical orientation has models, outlines, and checklists. Part three is a collection of quick-reference outline forms. Indexed.

650. Poe, Roy W. *The McGraw-Hill Handbook of Business Letters*. 2d ed. New York: McGraw-Hill, 1988. 306p.

The basic principles of good letter writing are considered, followed by model letters in thirteen areas. The book consists primarily of model letters: sales, transmittal, credit and collection, guest speakers, personnel and social correspondence. One section is devoted to interoffice memos, another to resumes and application letters. Each section contains explanation, analysis and sample letters. Indexed.

651. Poe, Roy W., and Fruehling, Rosemary T. *Business Communication: A Problem-Solving Approach*. 3d ed. New York: McGraw-Hill, 1984. 400p.

The problem-solving approach presents communications theory and practice for letters, memos and reports. There are illustrative case studies, model documents and examples of bad writing with possible solutions. The appendix supplies a glossary, word usage section, abbreviations and proofreaders' marks. A fourth edition is scheduled for publication in 1989. Indexed.

652. Reid, James M. Jr., and Silleck, Anne. *Better Business Letters*. 3d ed. Reading, MA: Addison-Wesley, 1985. 203p.

A self-instructional text, the six programmed lessons concentrate on developing writing skills and style through practice. The lessons have examples of letters. There are six quizzes, a diagnostic test, and answers in the appendices. Not indexed.

653. Robbins, Jane E. and Johnson, Kate L. *Contemporary Business Letters with Apple Writer II for the IIe*. Somerville MA: Curtin and London; New York: Van Nostrand Reinhold, 1984. 230p.

Form letters and techniques are furnished for using word processing to create letters. There are detailed instructions on the Apple Writer II program. The handbook format offers guidelines, tips, examples and hints for the Apple II in the appendix. Indexed.

654. Robbins, Larry M. *The Business of Writing and Speaking*. New York: McGraw-Hill, 1985. 223p.

The author concisely looks at oral and written communication principles and applications. The applications presented are letters, memos, proposals, reports, presentations, meetings and interviews (with samples). A glossary of style and usage appears in appendix one. Indexed.

655. Roman, Kenneth, and Raphaelson, Joel. *Writing That Works*. New York: Harper and Row, 1981. 105p.

This introduction to effective writing places examples of good writing next to examples of bad writing. The techniques support the preparation, with examples, of memo letters, reports and speeches. Not indexed.

656. Saville, Jenny, and Saville, Tim. *The Business Letter Writer*. London: Ward Lock, 1981. 175p.

The authors' brief guide explains the writing of sales, accounts, complaint and general business letters. There are checklists and model letters. Chapter seven displays other written documents such as memos and press releases. The book has a separate list of chapter sections and model letters. Not indexed.

657. Schell, John, and Stratton, John. *Writing On the Job: A Handbook for Business and Government*. New York: New American Library, 1984. 413p.

Clear instructions and examples are reported for creating letters, memos, proposals, reports and other documents. The text includes a discussion of writing in organizations and a guide to editing and style. Indexed.

658. Seglin, Jeffrey L. *Bank Letter Writing Handbook*. Boston: Bankers Publishing Company, 1983. 394p.

Instructions are combined with letter-writing guidelines. The eight categories of letters and one of memos emphasize letters written in financial institutions. There are over two hundred sample letters. The appendices examine words, grammar, abbreviations, and grammar hotlines. Not indexed.

659. Sharp, Deborah W. *Writing Business Letters with a Personal Touch.* Belmont, CA: Wadsworth Publishing Company, 1984. 288p.

In presenting guidelines for writing letters, the author considers over three hundred sample letters and memos. The letters are grouped in ten categories with samples, don'ts and checklists. Indexed.

660. Shurter, Robert L., and Leonard, Donald J. *Effective Letters in Business.* 3d ed. New York: McGraw-Hill, 1984. 238p.

Basic letter writing principles are applied to five kinds of letters, the resume and memos. The resume advice should be used cautiously as recent laws have eliminated age, sex and other personal factors from a resume. Indexed.

661. Starzyk, Lawrence J., and Jewell, John R. *Effective Business Writing.* New York: Macmillan, 1984. 342p.

Skills and strategies are supplied for composing letters, memos and reports. There are clear instructions and sample documents. A handbook of grammar and punctuation is in the appendix. Indexed.

662. Sterkel, Karen S. *Effective Business and Professional Letters.* Reston, VA: Reston Publishing Company, 1983. 177p.

The guidelines and checklists here address common, routine business situations, with models of letters and memos. Part one organizes writing by type of message while part two groups them by their area of business. The appendices serve as a handy reference guide by discussing usage, grammar and punctuation. Indexed.

663. Stout, Vickie J., and Perkins, Edward A. Jr. *Practical Management Communication.* Cincinnati, OH: South-Western Publishing Company, 1987. 406p.

The textbook concentrates on the development of listening, reading, writing and speaking skills. It highlights techniques (with models) for writing letters, memos, manuals and reports. A glossary and selected readings are in the appendices. Indexed.

664. Taylor, John R., and Bigger, Elise D. *The President's Letter Book.* Englewood Cliffs, NJ: Prentice-Hall, 1987. 197p.

Designed for chief executives, the letters are arranged according to the individuals addressed, for example, shareholders, government agencies and competitors. Some situations represented are unique to this book. There is a glossary of usage terms. Indexed.

665. Thomsett, Michael C. *The Little Black Book of Business Letters.* New York: AMACOM, 1988. 147p.

This is a brief examination of letter writing in business situations. It explains how to construct and format letters for different circumstances. Tips are given along with examples of different letters. Each chapter concludes with exercises, the answers for which are in the appendices. Appendix B is a quick check for punctuation and usage skills. Indexed.

666. Trace, Jacqueline. *Style and Strategy of the Business Letter.* Englewood Cliffs, NJ: Prentice-Hall, 1985. 176p.

The author has created a character, Robin Redgrave and, in following the character's career moves, demonstrates the basic principles of letter writing style and strategy. The many models are indicated in the list of illustrations. The appendices provide forms of address and abbreviations. Indexed.

667. Treece, Malra. *Successful Business Writing.* Boston: Allyn and Bacon, 1980. 412p.

Based on the author's longer book, *Communication for Business and the Professions,* writing theory with techniques and applications. For the letters, memos and reports discussed the models appear as figures in the text. Indexed.

668. Van Duyn, J. A., ed. *Director's and Officer's Complete Letter Book.* 2d ed. Edited by the Prentice-Hall Editorial Staff. Englewood Cliffs, NJ: Prentice-Hall, 1983. 303p.

Field-tested letters are furnished for executives, with description, rules, alternate phrasing and over one hundred models. The appendices have a master checklist and proper address forms. While there is no index, the table of contents is quite detailed. Not indexed.

669. Venolia, Jan. *Better Letters: A Handbook of Business and Personal Correspondence.* Berkeley, CA: Ten Speed Press; Periwinkle Press, 1981. 172p.

Style, format and the specifics of writing business and personal letters are studied. Some models are used as examples. Additional chapters consider non-sexist language and dictating. Expressions to avoid, abbreviations and forms of address are in the appendix. Indexed.

670. *Webster's Guide to Business Correspondence.* Springfield, MA: Merriam-Webster, 1988. 400p.

In this handbook of letter writing, style, grammar, mechanics and tone are reviewed with examples. Chapter six examines letter composition with over forty samples. The sample letters have a separate subject index. Problem areas such as forms of address, correspondence with the U.S. government, use of the postal service and the various aspects of handling correspondence are investigated. Indexed.

671. Wells, Walter. *Communications in Business.* 5th ed. Boston: PWS-Kent Publishing Company, 1988. 632p.

The fifth edition of this textbook continues the behavioral approach to development of written and oral communication skills. While the book emphasizes written communication, it also covers presentations and telephone usage. The text contains samples of proposals, minutes, agendas, resumes, letters and parts of reports. It discusses mechanics and "corpspeak", with a review of grammar in the appendices. A glossary of computer terms has been added to the glossary of business terms from the previous edition. Indexed.

MANUALS

672. American Society of Association Executives Foundation. *How to Write a Personnel Policy Manual: A Guide for the Association Executive.* Washington, DC: Foundation of the American Society of Association Executives, 1982. 40p.

For executives, this pamplet offers brief guidelines on writing effective personnel manuals. Model sections are placed next to the description of the content. A personnel policies checklist is in the appendix. Not indexed.

673. Brockman, R. John. *Writing Better Computer User Documentation. From Paper to Online.* New York: John Wiley and Sons, 1986. 289p.

The author presents a systematic approach to creating and updating user manuals. Designed for data processing professionals, parts two and three reveal a method for developing, editing and reviewing documentation. There are sample pages, checklists and examples of inadequate manuals. In part four the author discusses documentation created in computer rather than paper format. There is a glossary of terms. Indexed.

674. Brown, Harry L. *Design and Maintenance of Accounting Manuals.* New York: John Wiley and Sons, 1988. 269p.

Seven different accounting manuals are described with examples and sample forms. The text embraces three maintenance tools which can be utilized to update a manual. Several chapters stress writing style and mechanics. Indexed.

675. Browning, Christine. *Guide to Effective Software Technical Writing.* Englewood Cliffs, NJ: Prentice-Hall, 1984. 149p.

A step-by-step method, which does not assume a strong computer background, is advanced for writing software manuals. Useful to technical writers and other professionals as a general introduction, the how-to guide has numerous examples and a glossary. Indexed.

676. Crandall, Judith A. *How to Write Tutorial Documentation.* Englewood Cliffs, NJ: Prentice-Hall, 1987. 124p.

Basic instructional design principles are used to plan and write tutorial manuals. The book is organized according to the suggested structure, with examples and checklists. Each skill presented employs a five part lesson. Appendix A contains all the checklists for each chapter, appendix B the tutorial and reference guide for Miracalc. There is a glossary. Indexed.

677. Cunningham, Donald H., and Cohen, Gerald. *Creating Technical Manuals: A Step-by-Step Approach to Writing User-Friendly Instructions.* New York: McGraw-Hill, 1984. 160p.

The authors offer a series of plan sheets that can be photocopied and used to prepare a manual. The book focuses on procedures and product manuals but does not include samples or models. Indexed.

678. d'Agenais, Jean, and Carruthers, John. *Creating Effective Manuals.* Cincinnati, OH: South-Western Publishing Company, 1985. 274p.

The authors guide professionals through the stages of preparing a manual with step-by-step instructions and examples. The complex task of creating and producing employee and personnel manuals is simplified. Indexed.

679. Diamond, Susan Z. *Preparing Administrative Manuals.* New York: AMACOM, 1981. 133p.

Principles and guidelines are conveyed for producing different types of administrative manuals. Functions described are planning, producing, revising and securing manuals. The examples illustrate the text. Indexed.

680. Forbes, Mark. *Writing Technical Articles, Speeches and Manuals.* New York: John Wiley and Sons, 1988. 207p.

This technical writing book stresses use of the scientific method in writing papers for publication, technical manuals and presentations. The systematic method utilized employ outlining techniques and reduces writing tasks to subparts. The author offers pointers and examples but no sample documents. Indexed.

681. Grimm, Susan J. *How to Write Computer Documentation for Users.* 2d ed. New York: Van Nostrand Reinhold, 1987. 221p.

Practical procedures are outlined for planning, writing, reviewing, producing and maintaining user manuals. A chronological format is employed with many examples and checklists. The glossary and list of checklists add to the excellence of the author's approach to writing computer documentation. Indexed.

682. Holtz, Herman. *The Complete Guide to Writing Readable User Manuals.* Homewood, IL: Dow Jones-Irwin, 1988. 172p.

User instructions and manuals are planned and prepared with this brief guide. The basics of instructional writing and in-house publishing are advanced for instructions and training manuals. While there are no models, the many examples and outlines serve the same purpose. There is a brief glossary. Indexed.

683. Houghton-Alico, Doann. *Creating Computer Software User Guides: From Manuals to Menus.* New York: McGraw-Hill, 1985. 156p.

The development of effective user manuals is reviewed with examples and a glossary. The volume focuses on the planning stage. There are sample outlines, styles and formats for written manuals. Indexed.

684. Jacoby, James W. *How to Prepare Managerial Communications.* Washington, DC: Bureau of National Affairs, 1983. 232p.

Writing strategies are applied to the development and production of organizational, instructional and technical manuals. Appendix C features outlines of organizational, sales, purchasing policy and employee manuals. Indexed.

685. Katzin, Emanuel. *How to Write a Really Good User's Manual*. New York: Van Nostrand Reinhold, 1985. 249p.

The author employs a straight-forward approach to produce user documentation. A difficult subject is explained in a logical order with examples and samples from companies. The book should help the inexperienced write better user's manuals. Indexed.

686. Lunine, Leo R. *How to Research, Write, and Package Administrative Manuals*. New York: AMACOM, 1985. 317p.

Preparation of policy and procedure manuals is presented in chronological order. The emphasis is on program administration and company functions rather than how-to data. A sample evaluation checklist is included. Indexed.

687. McGehee, Brad. *The Complete Guide to Writing Software User Manuals*. Cincinnati, OH: Writer's Digest Books, 1984. 165p.

Volume unavailable for examination.

688. McQuaid, Robert W. *The Craft of Writing Technical Manuals*. R. W. McQuaid, 1983. 55p.

The self-study text contains the basic steps for creating a technical manual. Based on the author's experience, this brief volume is arranged in a non-threatening manner for trainees or classroom use. Not indexed.

689. Price, Jonathan. *How to Write a Computer Manual*. Menlo Park, CA: Benjamin/Cummings Publishing, 1984. 285p.

This is an easy to read introduction to creating, revising and testing user documentation. Developed at Apple Computer as a guide for new employees and freelance writers, the book stresses manuals for ordinary people rather than technical manuals for experts. There is a fifteen page checklist in an addendum. The appendices hold a sample style sheet and a glossary. Indexed.

690. Schoff, Gretchen H., and Robinson, Patricia A. *Writing and Designing Operator Manuals*. Belmont, CA: Lifetime Learning Publications, 1984. 162p.

Communication principles and practical guidelines are supplied for product manuals. The book is organized into the major steps with checklists and examples. Indexed.

691. Smock, Winston. *Technical Writing for Beginners*. Englewood Cliffs, NJ: Prentice-Hall, 1984. 167p.

For beginners, the author introduces scientific disciplines.There are detailed instructions for writing technical manuals. The text provides a glossary. Indexed.

692. Travis, A. B. *The Handbook Handbook*. New York: R. R. Bowker, 1984. 305p.

Comprehensive directions are given for policy and procedure handbooks and manuals. The easy to follow steps move from planning through development and implementation to maintenance. There are examples, forms and sample pages. A model handbook appears in the appendix. Indexed.

693. Weiss, Edmond H. *How to Write a Usable User Manual*. Philadelphia: ISI Press, 1985. 197p.

The style recommended for user manuals is used for the organization of the book. The planning, designing and writing techniques (with examples) describe what manuals do and how to approach writing them. A glossary and model table of contents are in the appendices. Indexed.

694. Zaneski, Richard. *Software Manual Production Simplified*. New York: Petrocelli Books, 1982. 190p.

Organized in the manner of a typical manual, production problems and their solutions are disclosed. Many examples and illustrations are used in showing how a manual evolves from mangement's initial philosophy. The book can function as a reference guide because of its step-by-step procedures. Indexed.

MARKETING PLAN

695. Bell, Martin L. *How to Prepare a Results-Driven Marketing Plan*. New York: AMACOM, 1987. 324p.

The procedure manual carefully guides the planner through the process of creating a marketing plan. Blank worksheets and a topic outline are available. The appendices include a situation analysis questionnaire and bibliography. Indexed.

696. Cohen, William A. *Developing a Winning Marketing Plan*. New York: John Wiley and Sons, 1987. 324p.

The purpose and elements are revealed for each segment of the marketing plan. Based on the author's research, the book examines a method for creating a professional plan with guidelines, examples, blank forms and worksheets. Two model plans are in appendix A. Indexed.

697. Hennessey, Hubert D. *How to Write a Marketing Plan*. New York: American Management Association, 1986. 179p.

Volume unavailable for examination.

698. Hopkins, David S. *The Marketing Plan*. New York: The Conference Board, 1981. 138p.

Survey research on marketing plans is summarized. The author provides guidelines, forms and schedules from specific companies. While the emphasis is on planning, the thirty-eight models in the exhibits section should be useful. Not indexed.

699. Luther, William M. *The Marketing Plan. How to Prepare and Implement It*. New York: AMACOM, 1982. 182p.

This book has objectives, strategies and plans for a ten-page marketing plan. The format of the plan is in chapter four. The conclusion is the key to using the book effectively. Indexed.

700. Makens, James C. *The Marketing Plan Workbook*. Englewood Cliffs, NJ: Prentice-Hall, 1985. 204p.

For marketing managers, a marketing plan can be formed with this workbook. The plan is broken into its component parts with blank worksheets for completion. The workbook does not have examples of completed pages. Not indexed.

701. Stapleton, John. *How to Prepare a Marketing Plan.* 3d ed. Aldershot, Hampshire, UK: Gower Publishing Company, 1982. 299p.

This marketing plan format emphasizes the planning process with many sample forms. The author encourages business people to develop customer-oriented marketing operations. Indexed.

MEMOS

702. Booher, Dianna. *Send Me a Memo. A Handbook of Model Memos.* New York: Facts on File, 1984. 201p.

Based on the five steps presented in the author's book, *How to Write Your Way to Success in Business*, fifty-two varieties of memos can be located through the table of contents. Each chapter supplies do's, don'ts and samples designed to produce concise, accurate written documentation. Not indexed.

703. Finn, Nancy B. *Writing Dynamics: A Guidebook to Written Communications in the Office of the 80's.* Boston: CBI Publishing Company, 1981. 157p.

This is a guide for managers to use in developing instruments of communication. It discusses different formats such as letters, memos, reports, proposals and presentations in detail with guidelines and many examples. Samples of letters and memos were obtained from specific companies. A separate handbook to grammar and usage appears as an appendix. Not indexed.

704. Fruehling, Rosemary T., and Bouchard, Sharon. *Business Correspondence: Essentials of Communication.* 4th ed. New York: McGraw-Hill, 1986. 204p.

Entitled *Business Correspondence/30* in earlier editions, this is a short course in the basics of letter, memo and report writing in a workbook format. Only one small chapter concerns the preparation of reports. A separate reference section summarizes punctuation, abbreviations and capitaliztion styles. Indexed.

705. Gilsdorf, Jeannette W. *Business Correspondence for Today: Letters, Memos, and Short Reports.* New York: John Wiley and Sons, 1989. 398p.

Volume unavailable for examination.

706. Hochheiser, Robert M. *Don't State It... Communicate It! How to Put Clout in Your Letters, Memos, Reports and Proposals.* Woodbury, NY: Barron's Educational Series, 1985. 183p.

Techniques for persuasive writing are applied to letters, memos, reports and other documents. The main elements of a business plan are briefly debated. Chapter ten involves editing. Indexed.

707. Holcombe, Marya W., and Stein, Judith K. *Writing for Decision Makers.* 2d ed. New York: Van Nostrand Reinhold, 1987. 219p.

The authors shows how to plan, organize and write memos and reports. The practical course features guidelines and criteria but very little grammar. The text covers writing with a word processor and case studies with solutions. Indexed.

708. Lesikar, Raymond V. *Basic Business Communication.* 4th ed. Homewood, IL: Irwin, 1988. 680p.

Volume unavailable for examination.

709. Reimold, Cheryl. *How to Write a Million Dollar Memo.* New York: Dell Publishing Company, 1984. 118p.

The author proposes a system for writing clear and simple memos that are persuasive, interesting and informative. Then the same techniques are put to use in writing letters, proposals and reports. This is a brief guide with examples. Not indexed.

710. Roddick, Ellen. *Writing That Means Business: A Manager's Guide.* New York: Macmillan, 1984. 120p.

This guide to writing letters, memos and reports introduces ways to handle language effectively. There are outlines, checklists and examples for each key point. Indexed.

711. Sweetnam, Sherry. *The Executive Memo. A Guide to Persuasive Business Communications.* New York: John Wiley and Sons, 1986. 248p.

Letters, memos, reports and proposals are written with communication and sales methods. Writing is seen as a marketing tool for managers. The book has checklists and model documents. Indexed.

712. Swindle, Robert E. *The Concise Business Correspondence Style Guide.* Englewood Cliffs, NJ: Prentice-Hall, 1983. 312p.

The guide to effective memos, letters and reports discusses the rules of writing, provides careful checklists and examples. There are samples of letters and reports. Indexed.

713. VanHuss, Susie H. *Basic Letter and Memo Writing.* Cincinnati, OH: South-Western Publishing Company, 1981. 188p.

In the workbook, writing principles are combined with application chapters. The ten easy guides to letters and memos have examples and exercises. Models appear in the text as examples. Not indexed.

714. Westheimer, Patricia H. *The Perfect Memo.* Glenview, IL: Scott Foresman, 1988. 193p.

The Speakwrite system uses five steps to construct memos and other written documents. The system concentrates on streamlining the writing process through formulas and guidelines. The book has numerous examples. The appendix examines usage and wording choices. Indexed.

715. Westheimer, Patricia H. *Power Writing for Executive Women.* Glenview, IL: Scott Foresman, 1989. 208p.

Volume unavailable for examination.

NEWSLETTERS

716. Arth, Marvin, and Ashmore, Helen. *The Newsletter Editor's Desk Book*. 3d ed. Shawnee Mission, KS: Parkway Press, 1984. 178p.

The production of newsletters and special-audience periodicals is described along with a review of applicable journalism principles. For editors, the book answers questions on organizing, editing, formatting, and producing. The appendices contain several models, forms, formula stories, and proofreading marks. The detailed table of contents makes accessing this volume easy. Indexed.

717. Beach, Mark. *Editing Your Newsletter*. 2d ed. New York: Van Nostrand Reinhold, 1982. 122p.

Organized around the twelve questions faced by all editors, the book assumes little training in writing and editing newsletters. The practical, how-to manual offers guidelines and techniques for newsletters, brochures and bulletins. Indexed.

718. Brigham, Nancy; Raszmann, Ann; and Babson, Steve. *How to do Leaflets, Newsletters and Newspapers*. Boston: PEP Publishers, 1982. 144p.

How to create leaflets and newsletters is demonstrated through discussion, example, and referral to other sources. The forty-eight key pages indicated in the table of contents should be read first. Terms are defined as they appear in the text and are listed in the index. The author's approach is very practical, although the busy layout is confusing. Indexed.

719. Reid, Gerene. *How to Write Company Newsletters*. 2d ed. Margate, FL: TIB Publications, 1980. 80p.

This is a brief guide to writing sales, employee and customer newsletters. The book emphasizes how to write, not how to produce a newsletter. Not indexed.

PROPOSALS

720. Bell, Arthur H. *Business Communication: Process and Practice*. Glenview, IL: Scott Foresman, 1987. 601p.

Numerous case studies are used to present written and oral business communication. Instructions are furnished for writing letters, memos, proposals and reports, with models. Oral skills investigated are listening, meeting and oral presentations. A guide to grammar and usage is in the appendix. Indexed.

721. Helgeson, Donald V. *Handbook for Writing Technical Proposals That Win Contracts*. Englewood Cliffs, NJ: Prentice-Hall, 1985. 218p.

Procedures for the preparation of research and development proposals are unveiled. The text, which emphasizes preparation and evaluation of a sales document, has guidelines, practical advice, and sample outlines. Indexed.

722. Hillman, Howard. *The Art of Writing Business Reports and Proposals*. New York: Vanguard Press, 1981. 230p.

Field-tested tips are contained in a self-teaching guide. In considering report and proposal writing, the author cites advice, six samples, a bibliography and an annotated guide to information sources. Not indexed.

723. Holtz, Herman. *The Consultant's Guide to Proposal Writing*. New York: John Wiley and Sons, 1986. 294p.

The author is concerned with developing, writing and using proposals as a marketing tool. While the emphasis is on marketing skills rather than writing skills, the book does cover design, graphics, summaries and other concerns. The suggested standard formats in chapter thirteen refer to figures scattered throughout the book. Indexed.

724. Holtz, Herman. *Persuasive Writing*. New York: McGraw-Hill, 1983. 238p.

Methodologies are presented for writing persuasive sales documents such as proposals, newsletters and direct mail. The book highlights written communication with few models. Indexed.

725. Holtz, Herman, and Schmidt, Terry. *The Winning Proposal. How to Write It*. New York: McGraw-Hill, 1981. 381p.

Developing proposals for U.S. government contracts is studied here. The text contains a sample proposal, sample government forms and glossary for guidance. Indexed.

726. Lannon, John M. *Technical Writing*. 3d ed. Boston: Little, Brown and Company, 1985. 604p.

This introduction to skill development emphasizes the process of writing before the product. Criteria and guidelines are implemented through revision checklists and illustrative models (letters, proposals, reports and presentations). A review of grammar and usage is in appendix A. The fourth edition is due for publication in 1988. Indexed.

727. Loring, Roy, and Kerzner, Harold. *Proposal Preparation and Management Handbook*. New York: Van Nostrand Reinhold, 1982. 430p.

Proposals are organized, prepared and managed during the management process. Elements of a proposal and the different kinds are reviewed. This book is most useful in the development of project proposals which require management, technical and cost information for completion. A preparation checklist and evaluation considerations are in the appendices. Indexed.

728. Meador, Roy. *Guidelines for Preparing Proposals*. Chelsea, MI: Lewis Publishers, 1985. 116p.

Based on the author's experience, guidelines are communicated for organizing, compiling and writing proposals for grants, venture capital and R & D projects. The business plan is shown in chapter eight, sample proposals in chapter ten. A list of examples and a bibliography are included. Indexed.

729. Mills, Gordon H., and Walter, John A. *Technical Writing*. 5th ed. New York: Holt Rinehart and Winston, 1986. 554p

The textbook introduces technical writing techniques for letters, proposals and reports. Chapters report how to organize and prepare a document and feature a model of each. There is an extensive bibliography of research materials in business and engineering. Indexed.

730. Persing, Bobbye S. *Business Communication Dynamics*. Columbus, OH: Charles E. Merrill, 1981. 760p.

Communication theory is related to oral and written communication in this textbook. The book advances guidelines, numerous examples and exercises in a systems approach (for reports, memos, letters, proposals, resumes, listening and speaking). A sample proposal and report appear in the appendices. Indexed.

731. Pfeiffer, William S. *Proposal Writing: The Art of Friendly Persuasion*. Columbus, OH: Merrill Publishing Company, 1989. 230p.

Volume unavailable for examination.

732. Porter-Roth, Bud. *Proposal Development: A Winning Approach*. Milpitas, CA: Oasis Press, 1986. 174p.

The mechanics of proposal preparation are practiced with examples. The separate list of illustrations leads to the checklists, guidelines and sample forms. The appendices display three sample letters and seven blank reproducible forms. Not indexed.

733. Roetzheim, William H. *Proposal Writing for the Data Processing Consultant*. Englewood Cliffs, NJ: Prentice-Hall, 1986. 229p.

Writing and presenting, for technical, management and cost proposals, features formal marketing procedures. The book is comprised of useful checklists, outlines and advice. Sample government forms are in appendix C. Not indexed.

734. Stewart, Rodney D., and Stewart, Ann L. *Proposal Preparation*. New York: John Wiley and Sons, 1984. 319p.

This proposal handbook presents the elements of the proposal writing process. How to create a company proposal manual or team is examined with outlines, checklists and a sample proposal manual. The table of contents serves as an outline of a proposal. Chapter twelve is a case study/sample proposal. Indexed.

735. Tepper, R., ed. *How to Write Winning Proposals for Your Company or Client*. New York: John Wiley and Sons, 1989. 269p.

Writing and presenting proposals is fostered through the insights of nineteen top proposal writers, case histories and copies of actual proposals. The focus is on RFPs, grants, R & D funds, and private and government grants. Directions are given for preparing verbal proposals and presentations. Indexed.

736. Whalen, Tim. *Preparing Contract-Winning Proposals*. New York: Pilot Books, 1982. 48p.

The author briefly presents the process and methodology for developing proposals and feasibility studies. The methodology described can be adjusted for a special business or request for proposal (RFP). The no-nonsense approach supports the basics with little elaboration besides checklists and charts. Not indexed.

737. Whalen, Timothy. *Writing and Managing Winning Technical Proposals.* Boston: Artech House, 1987. 239p.

The process of planning and writing competitive proposals is investigated. The text features an outline, writing plan and detailed checklist. The guidelines can be modified to meet the specific needs of a request for proposal (RFP). There is a chapter of related readings and an extensive bibliography. Not indexed.

REPORTS

738. Anderson, W. Steve, and Cox, Don R. *The Technical Reader.* 2d ed. New York: Holt, Rinehart and Winston, 1984. 357p.

This selection of readings consists largely of reprinted articles and book chapters. The articles concern the creation of technical documents, particularly reports. Model documentss can be found in part three. Indexed.

739. Andrews, Deborah C., and Blickle, Margaret D. *Technical Writing: Principles and Forms.* 2d ed. New York: Macmillan; London: Collier Macmillan, 1982. 455p.

Written communication is emphasized here. The textbook reviews letters, resumes, abstracts, proposals, reports, oral reports and meetings with numerous examples and exercises. There are samples of the letter, abstract, proposal, resumes and a complete final report. Section three is a handbook on usage. Indexed.

740. Barnett, Marva T. *Writing for Technicians.* Albany, NY: Delmar Publishers, 1982. 358p.

Technical writing fundamentals and English usage are introduced for professionals. A direct style is used in presenting guidelines and techniques for writing letters and reports. Sample letters, proposal, and short reports appear as figures in the text. The third edition was published in 1987. Indexed.

741. Barr, Doris W. *Communication for Business, Professional, and Technical Students.* 2d ed. Belmont, CA: Wadsworth Publishing Company, 1980. 495p.

After introducing basic communication forms, problem situations and their solutions are considered. Problems are resolved through effective reports, letters, listening and interviewing. Examples are provided in the text. Chapter thirteen on interpreting data is unique for this kind of textbook. The technical review at the end of the book is a handbook of exercises, grammar and usage. Indexed.

742. Baxter, Carol M. *Business Report Writing: A Practical Approach.* Boston: Kent Publishing Company, 1983. 373p.

Report writing theory and practice is demonstrated using numerous examples. For students and management trainees, chapters include learning objectves and activities. The three-part book discloses the elements of report writing, managerial reports, and special reports such as an annual report. Samples of the different reports appear as figures and are in the list of illustrations. A glossary and brief guide to usage are available. Indexed.

743. Blicq, Ron S. *Guidelines for Report Writing. A Complete Manual for On-the-Job Report Writing.* Englewood Cliffs, NJ: Prentice-Hall, 1982. 182p.

The pyramid technique, a modular method of report organization, is described. With it and samples of the various reports, reports (informal, semi-formal and formal) and proposals can be created. This is meant to serve as a ready-reference handbook with guidelines. Indexed.

744. Bonner, William H. *Communicating in Business: Key to Sucess.* 4th ed. Houston, TX: Dame Publications, 1986. 560p.

The development of oral and written skills progresses from easy messages to the more difficult ones. In five parts the book features style, letters, reports, word processing and oral communications (meetings, speeches, instructions and telephone calls). There are samples of the written documents. Part six is a grammar and usage handbook. Indexed.

745. Booher, Dianna. *How to Write Your Way to Success in Business.* New York: Barnes and Noble, 1984. 133p.

Written in the form of a business report, the author identifies five steps necessary for effective reports, letters and memos. These steps are discussed in detail with examples, exercises, quizzes and a grammar glossary. The book was originally published in 1983 as *Would You Put That in Writing?* Not indexed.

746. Bowbrick, Peter. *Effective Communication for Professionals and Executives.* London: Graham and Trotman, 1988. 135p.

This introduction for professionals applies basic oral and written skills in specific situations. Publishing, reviewing concerns, and creating a curriculum vitae are highlighted. The book briefly considers writing reports and giving talks but does not have any sample documents. A chapter is devoted to speaking on the radio rather than on television. Indexed.

747. Bowman, Joel P., and Branchaw, Bernadine P. *Business Report Writing.* 2d ed. Chicago: Dryden Press, 1988. 607p.

Written reports are stressed here. The textbook implements research methodology and presentation strategies in report writing. Planning checklists and sample documents are conveyed for proposals, resumes and different reports: annual, feasibility, memorandum, analytical and progress reports. Samples appear as figures in the text. Resumes and the job application process are discussed in Appendix C. Indexed.

748. Brinegar, Bonnie C., and Skates, Craig B. *Technical Writing.* Glenview, IL: Scott Foresman, 1983. 349p.

Descriptions of fifteen different professional documents and reports are combined with over forty models in an introduction to technical writing. The organizational setting of each model is explained with suggested applications. While designed for students, practitioners in business and technical fields will find this approach useful. Access is provided through a detailed table of contents, index and a list of models. Indexed.

749. Brown, Harry M. *Business Report Writing.* New York: Van Nostrand, 1980. 350p.

Professionals can acquire report writing skills through completion of the exercises and problems in this book. Models of proposals and reports (chapters ten and eleven) are included with discussion of construction, content and graphics. Indexed.

750. Brown, John F. *A Student Guide to Engineering Report Writing.* 2d ed. Solana Beach, CA: United Western Press, 1985. 171p.

This basic text for students on report preparation was developed from the author's lecture notes. While other works provide a more detailed explanation of report writing, chapter eleven promotes the author's correction code used in correcting student papers. The code enables students and practitioners to avoid common report-writing mistakes. The second edition contains sample laboratory reports and a chapter on handling equations. Indexed.

751. Brown, Leland. *Effective Business Report Writing.* 4th ed. Englewood Cliffs, NJ: Prentice-Hall, 1985. 415p.

The fourth edition has been revised into three sections: theory, function of reports, and preparation. The major elements of the report writing process are deliberated in order to stimulate professionals. The index assists in the location of discussions, checklists and models of annual reports, questionnaires and specialty reports. Problems, exercises and case studies support use of the volume as a textbook. There is a handbook of grammar and usage in appendix A. Indexed.

752. Brunner, Ingrid; Mathes, J. C.; and Stevenson, Dwight W. *The Technician as Writer. Preparing Technical Reports.* Indianapolis, IN: Bobbs-Merrill, 1980. 231p.

Effective reports are designed in a systematic manner. While aimed at tehcnicians, chapter nine, in reviewing all aspects of the report writing process, is applicable in other situations. There are models of production reports and other specialized documents. The index and list of figures promote the usefulness of this volume. Indexed.

753. Carosso, Rebecca B. *Technical Communication.* Belmont, CA: Wadsworth Publishing Company, 1986. 622p.

Basically a textbook for students and professionals, the applications chapters discuss abstracts, manuals, proposals, oral presentations and several kinds of reports. Sample documents are listed in both the table of contents and the index. A separate usage handbook summarizes key points in figures and checklists. Indexed.

754. Carr-Ruffino, Norma. *Writing Short Business Reports*. New York: McGraw-Hill, 1980. 194p.

Divided into learning units, the textbook considers the basic principles and techniques to be employed in planning, organizing and writing short reports. Some of the units have workbook-like spaces for answering the exercises. There are examples but no sample reports. The appendices provide symbols for correcting reports. Indexed.

755. Comeau, John, and Diehn, Gwen. *Communication on the Job: A Practical Approach*. Englewood Cliffs, NJ: Prentice-Hall, 1987. 356p.

The authors advance communications theory, practical applications and a discussion of grammar and style. Designed for a variety of classes, letters, memos and reports are studied. There are exercises and model documents. A chapter is devoted to listening and speaking skills. Indexed.

756. Damerst, William A. *Clear Technical Reports*. 2d ed. New York: HBJ Media Systems, 1982. 325p.

The basic principles of communication are applied to preparing letters, memos, reports and presentations. The text supplies exercises and model documents. Part three consists of a handbook to punctuation, grammar, spelling and abbreviations. Indexed.

757. Felker, Daniel B., et al. *Guidelines for Document Designers*. Washington, DC: American Institutes for Research, 1981. 117p.

Designed as a desk reference, twenty-five principles are used in creating clearer and easier to understand public documents. This product of the Document Design Project stresses how-to information such as guidelines and examples of poor and good writing. The lack of an index makes use as a handbook difficult . Not indexed.

758. Foreman, Robert L. *Communicating the Appraisal: A Guide to Report Writing*. Chicago: American Institute of Real Estate Appraisers, 1982. 85p.

After describing the appraisal report and its reporting requirements, the author relates guidelines and examples of the letter, form, and narrative reports. The book is used to train appraisers in conjunction with the Institute's training course. Not indexed.

759. Gallagher, William J. *Writing the Business and Technical Report*. Boston: CBI Publishing Company, 1981. 149p.

This volume functions as a self-teaching guide to writing reports with numerous examples . Answers to the exercises are in the appendices with a guide to grammar, references and bibliography. The lack of an index complicates a search for specific aspects of the report writing process. Not indexed.

760. Gelderman, Carol. *Better Writing for Professionals. A Concise Guide*. Glenview, IL: Scott Foresman, 1984. 116p.

In a brief, handy reference, professionals can follow the process for writing articles, speeches, reports, letters and memos. Chapters provide examples along with the do's and don'ts. A sample short report is available. The checklists are listed in the index. Indexed.

761. Golen, Steven P.; Pearce, C. Glenn; and Figgins, Ross. *Report Writing for Business and Industry*. New York: John Wiley and Sons, 1985. 526p.

The authors emphasize the planning, procedures and techniques necessary in writing reports. The special reports shown are proposals, annual reports, and policy or procedure manuals. There are models of the different documents. Part five entails using word processing and making oral presentations. Elements of grammar, a glossary and letter and memo formats are in the six appendices. Indexed.

762. Goodman, Michael B. *Write to the Point. Effective Communication in the Workplace*. Englewood Cliffs, NJ: Prentice-Hall, 1984. 364p.

Developed from the author's seminar work, the book focuses on the development of clear and direct writing skills in the workplace. Checklists and examples support instruction for letters, memos, proposals, reports and presentations. A sample report appears in Appendix B. Indexed.

763. Harcourt, Jules; Krizan, A. C.; and Merrier, Patricia. *Business Communication*. Cincinnati, OH: South-Western Publishing Company, 1987. 501p.

The text conveys the fundamentals of communication, grammar and style. Letters, memos, and reports are constructed with examples and a sample long report. The textbook also studies listening and international business. Indexed.

764. Houp, Kenneth W., and Pearsall, Thomas E. *Reporting Technical Information*. 6th ed. New York: Macmillan; London: Collier Macmillan, 1988. 596p.

In the new edition of a technical writing textbook, basic writing principles and techniques are applied in writing letters, proposals, instructions and feasibility reports. Most of the sample documents (letters, progress report, resume, project summary) are indicated in the table of contents. Part four is a handbook of grammar, usage, punctuation and mechanics. A complete student report is in the appendix. Indexed.

765. Huseman, Richard C.; Lahiff, James M.; and Penrose, John M. Jr. *Business Communication: Strategies and Skills*. 3d ed. Chicago: Dryden Press, 1988. 702p.

The textbook employs a practical approach to written and oral communication. The authors advance strategies for fashioning letters, long reports, memos, short reports, policies and procedures, presentations and interviewing. The book has checklists for oral skills, models for written ones, and guidelines for grammar, punctuation and usage. Indexed.

766. Iacone, Salvatore J. *Modern Business Report Writing*. New York: Macmillan; London: Collier Macmillan, 1985. 380p.

A practical guide to preparing reports, the book combines theory with step-by-step directions for preparing a report. There are many samples in the text and the appendices. How to write an abstract and prepare an oral report are also disclosed. Chapter twelve is an English usage handbook. Indexed.

767. Iyer, Venkata. *Writing Readable Business Reports*. New Delhi, India: Sterling; New York: APT Books, 1988. 76p.
Volume unavailable for examination.

768. Lawrence, Nelda R., and Tebeaux, Elizabeth. *Writing Communications in Business and Industry*. 3d ed. Englewood Cliffs, NJ: Prentice-Hall, 1982. 254p.
Style, letters, memos, graphics and reports are presented in a workbook format. Realistic problems and exercises promote skill development. There are sample reports, proposals and examples of both good and bad writing. Indexed.

769. Lesikar, Raymond V. *How to Write a Report Your Boss Will Read and Remember*. rev ed. Homewood, IL: Dow Jones-Irwin, 1984. 223p.
The author offers principles and procedures for writing effective reports. Models of five reports are in the appendices along with guides to correctness and documentation. Indexed.

770. Lesikar, Raymond V., and Lyons, Mary P. *Report Writing for Business*. 7th ed. Homewood, IL: Richard D. Irwin, 1986. 421p.
The textbook describes the steps in report writing with examples, margin notes and exercises. Oral reports are prepared in part six. The appendices include a checklist, sampling techniques, two tests and several model reports. Indexed.

771. Level, Dale A. Jr., and Galle, William P. Jr. *Business Communication: Theory and Practice*. Dallas, TX: Business Publications; Georgetown: Ontario, Irwin-Dorsey, 1980. 400p.
The basic principles of communication appear first in this textbook. The communication skills covered are: letters, reports, manuals, interviews, listening and reports. Sample letters and interview questions are in the text. There are exercises for each skill discussed. The appendices contain a discussion of resumes, a sample employment interview and models of a formal and memorandum report. Indexed.

772. Lewis, Phillip, and Baker, William H. *Business Report Writing*. 2d ed. Columbus, OH: Grid Publishing, 1983. 368p.
Research methodology and the report writing process are examined. Accompanying the report writing principles are practical instructions and checklists for both written and oral reports. Sample reports appear as exhibits in the text, sample resumes in Appendix B. Indexed.

773. MacKenzie, Raymond N., and Evans, William E. *Technical Writing: Forms and Formats*. Dubuque, IA: Kendall/Hunt Publishing, 1982. 168p.
This technical writing textbook has thirty student papers and reports arranged in a progressive order of compexity. Chapters offer checklists and sample papers. Not indexed.

774. Monroe, Jud. *Effective Research and Report Writing in Government*. New York: McGraw-Hill, 1980. 289p.

The guidelines here can be used in developing and conducting a study and presenting the results. While the book emphasizes research rather than writing, the procedural suggestions and the advice on thinking through each stage are valuable. Indexed.

775. Monroe, Jud, and Fisher, Judith E. *A Short Course in Effective Research and Report Writing in Government.* New York: McGraw-Hill, 1980. 132p.

A self-paced course in conducting research and writing reports is related in a workbook. It takes the reader through planning, conducting research, analyzing data and writing a report. Practice is accomplished through exercises (with answers) and a checklist (for revising, editing and reviewing). Not indexed.

776. Moore, Nick, and Hesp, Martin. *The Basics of Writing Reports Etcetera.* London: Clive Bingley, 1985. 109p.

The book identifies types of reports and shows how to produce appropriate, clearly written documents. Areas covered are annual reports, press releases, brochures, research reports, internal reports and meeting minutes. Indexed.

777. Moroney, Mary H. *You Can Write a Winning Report.* Westbury, NY: Caddylak Publishing, 1984. 37p.

This is a brief compilation of forms and checklists for writing reports. The author outlines the techniques and steps to follow. The steps are those displayed in the planning form. The appendix guides writing skill improvement through misused, misspelled words and punctuation pointers. Not indexed.

778. Mort, Simon. *How to Write a Successful Report.* London: Business Books, 1983. 280p.

Report writing is seen here as an art form. The guidelines and examples are applicable to work situations in England. Part three on special reports handles appraisal reports, abstracts and telexed reports. Frequent reference is made to articles and correspondence in *The Spectator.* Indexed.

779. Moyer, Ruth; Stevens, Eleanour; and Switzer, Ralph. *The Research and Report Handbook for Business, Industry, and Government.* student ed. New York: John Wiley and Sons, 1981. 312p.

The report writing process is reviewed with examples and models of short documents. Also published under the title, *The Research and Report Handbook for Managers and Executives in Business, Industry and Government*, the book emphasizes research. In the first two parts, each chapter discloses the purpose and organization of a document with examples. Parts five and six consist of government and business information sources. Part seven is a guide to style through capitalization and punctuation. Indexed.

780. Munter, Mary. *Business Communication: Strategy and Skill.* Englewood Cliffs, NJ: Prentice-Hall, 1987. 493p.

The author teaches strategies for developing letters, memos, reports, presentations and meetings. There are examples, checklists, techniques and models of written forms. The appendices feature grammar, punctuation, word usage and an excellent bibliography of business reference sources. Indexed.

781. Murdock, Michael L. *Writing Clearly and Effectively.* 2d ed. Washington, DC: Transemantics, 1987. 172p.

Volume unavailable for examination.

782. Pearce, C. Glenn; Figgins, Ross; and Golen, Steven P. *Business Communication: Theory and Practice.* 2d ed. New York: John Wiley and Sons, 1988. 746p.

This textbook acquaints students with word processing skills, letters, memos, proposals, reports, resumes, interviewing, meetings, conferences, presentations and listening. There are numerous examples, checklists and models of letters, memos, proposals, a formal reports and the resume. Among the many appendices are a review of grammar and a good bibliography of business reference sources. Indexed.

783. Poe, Roy W. *The McGraw-Hill Guide to Effective Business Reports.* New York: McGraw-Hill, 1982. 208p.

Writing of formal and informal reports is communication in a self-study guide, with exercises and answers. The guidelines and models support the creation of effective reports. There is a separate discussion of letter reports. Indexed.

784. Rivers, William E., ed. *Business Reports: Samples from the "Real World."* Selected and Introduced by William E. Rivers. Englewood Cliffs, NJ: Prentice-Hall, 1981. 262p.

This collection of thirty-eight sample reports serves as a book of readings or a supplemental text for students. The assignments assist the discussion of report content, style and organization. While some selections are slightly out-of-date, this does not hamper the overall effectivness of this view of report writing in the business world. Indexed.

785. Ruch, William V., and Crawford, Maurice L. *Business Reports: Written and Oral.* Boston: PWS-Kent Publishing Company, 1988. 388p.

The textbook, in emphasizing the creation of effective oral and written reports, concentrates on improving skills with examples, review questions, exercises and case studies. Sample reports appear as textual figures and feature formal, informal, progress and recommendation reports. Indexed.

786. Rutherfoord, Andrea J. *Basic Communication Skills for Electronics Technology.* Englewood Cliffs, NJ: Prentice-Hall, 1989. 332p.

The use of technical vocabulary and concepts is pointed up in a review of technical report planning and writing. Basic business letters are given with examples. Chapters consist of a reading (reprinted from another source), review questions, and exercises. Parts five and six are a workbook on grammar and mechanics. A concise model of the technical report appears in Appendix three; word processing tips, symbols and misused words in the other appendices. Indexed.

787. Schmidt, Steven. *Creating the Technical Report.* Englewood Cliffs, NJ: Prentice-Hall, 1983. 159p.

The process of producing a report is revealed for those employed in industry. The book offers examples and sample pages, but does not have any review questions, discussion topics or assignments. There is a glossary. Indexed.

788. Seigle, Natalie R. *Dynamics of Business Communications*. New York: John Wiley and Sons, 1984. 517p.

Applicable for middle-management, the textbook teaches the basics of written and oral communication. Communication theory is applied to letters, reports, memos, presentations, and listening. A sample formal report is in the appendix. Indexed.

789. Sides, Charles H. *How to Write Papers and Reports About Computer Technology*. Philadelphia: ISI Press, 1984. 142p.

The author's guidelines and instructions aid in the preparation of memos, specifications, procedures, proposals, different kinds of reports and oral presentations. The book takes a practical look at the process with examples. Indexed.

790. Sigband, Norman B., and Bateman, David N. *Communicating in Business*. 2d ed. Glenview, IL: Scott Foresman, 1985. 590p.

The textbook uses margin notes, questions and exercises. Skills stressed are discussing, planning, outlining, writing and revising. The book covers memos, letters, reports, speeches, listening, interviewing, meetings, conferences and resumes. A sample report appears in the appendix. The third edition should be available in 1989. Indexed.

791. Sigband, Norman B., and Bell, Arthur H. *Communication for Management and Business*. 4th ed. Glenview, IL: Scott Foresman, 1986. 892p.

Traditional and nontraditional areas of oral and written communication are debated with problems, exercises, examples and models of the written forms. The text explains letters, memos, reports, listening, interviews, meetings and presentations (with sample letters and reports). There are sixteen cases, twelve reprinted readings and a guide to usage in the appendix. Indexed.

792. Skees, William D. *Writing Handbook for Computer Professionals*. Belmont, CA: Lifetime Learning Publications, 1982. 296p.

Guidance is given here for writing data processing documents, technical documents, management budgets, reports, promotional newsletters, brochures and proposals. The examples highlight on-the-job writing in the computer field. The models are indicated in the chapter outlines. Indexed.

793. Smeltzer, Larry R., and Waltman, John L. *Managerial Communication: A Strategic Approach*. New York: John Wiley and Sons, 1984. 556p.

This communications textbook for managers employs chapter questions and exercises. Strategies and guidelines are put to use in creating letters, memos and reports (with a model report). The discussion of oral skills conveys methods for improving listening and interviewing. There is a glossary. Indexed.

794. Sussams, John E. *How to Write Effective Reports*. Aldershot, Hants, UK: Gower Publishing Company, 1983. 109p.

Report writing is introduced. The author relates the purpose and structure of a report, emphasizing layout, revising, punctuation and planning. There are no sample documents, but there are exercises at the back of the book. Not indexed.

795. Swenson, Dan H. *Business Reporting: A Management Tool.* Chicago: Science Research Associates, 1983. 500p.

This textbook focuses on skills needed for writing and presenting effective reports. Assistance appears in the guise of case studies and model documents (as textual figures). The appendices include formats, exercise answers, sample topics, and reference material. Indexed.

796. Thomsett, Michael C. *The Little Black Book of Business Reports.* New York: AMACOM, 1988. 162p.

Creation of effective business reports is supported by guidelines, examples, work projects (with solutions) and samples of the different kinds of reports. There is a quick guide to punctuation and usage in the appendices. Indexed.

797. Treece, Malra. *Communication for Business and the Professions.* 3d ed. Boston: Allyn and Bacon, 1986. 608p.

Theory, techniques and applications are communicated for letters, memos, resumes, reports, listening, interviewing and presentations. Model documents appear as textual figures, including a sample formal report. Some examples are indicated in the index and the table of contents. The appendices cover formats, style manuals, legal considerations and usage briefly. Indexed.

798. Treece, Malra. *Effective Reports.* 2d ed. Boston: Allyn and Bacon, 1985. 545p.

Designed as a textbook, extensive guidelines and detailed instructions are presented for preparing oral and written reports. The interrelatedness of the elements of communication is stressed. The author provides sample reports. Dictation considerations, cases and a brief guide to usage are in the appendices. Indexed.

799. Treece, Malra. *Successful Business Communication.* 3d ed. Boston: Allyn and Bacon, 1987. 511p.

The business communications textbook, in handling written communication, contains exercises and models of letters, memos, resumes and short reports. The book elaborates on listening and presentation skills. A sample long, formal report and a guide to usage are among the five appendices. Parts of the book also appeared in *Communication for Business and the Professions.* Indexed.

800. Trzyna, Thomas N., and Batschelet, Margaret W. *The Technical Writing Casebook.* Belmont, CA: Wadsworth Publishing Company, 1988. 200p.

The thirty short cases are meant to supplement the authors' text or a similar textbook. Basic principles of both technical writing and business comunication are cited. The cases explore letters, reports, instructions, manuals, proposals and brochures. Chapter two explains how to use the cases, some of which have model documents. The book could be used for independent study. Indexed.

801. Van Duyn, J. *The DP Professional's Guide to Writing Effective Technical Communications*. New York: John Wiley and Sons, 1982. 218p.

Descriptions of proposal and report writing procedures are combined with many examples and models. While the emphasis is on system-related documents, the guidelines are applicable to other situations. There is a useful section on writing mechanics. Indexed.

802. Varner, Iris I. *Contemporary Business Report Writing*. Chicago: Dryden Press, 1987. 466p.

All aspects of the report writing process are discussed in this textbook. Most chapters examine written reports but chapter sixteen covers oral ones. There are step-by-step directions for long, formal reports in chapters six through fifteen. A sample report is in the appendix to chapter fifteen. The samples can be located through the very detailed index. Indexed.

803. Warren, Thomas L. *Technical Writing: Purpose, Process, and Form*. Belmont, CA: Wadsworth Publishing Company, 1985. 344p.

Chapters in this work parallel the steps involved in the report writing process. Other technical forms studied are letters, abstracts, proposals, memos and presentations (with some examples). There is a sample student report in the appendices as well as a discussion of documentation, grammar and mechanics. Indexed.

804. Weisman, Herman M. *Basic Technical Writing*. 5th ed. Columbus, OH: Charles E. Merrill, 1985. 479p.

This technical writing textbook offers extensive coverage of reports, proposals and correspondence. Chapter eighteen is on oral reports. The student and professional examples can be located through the index. Part five adds a guide to grammar and usage and an extensive bibliography of related mateials. Indexed.

805. Weiss, Allen. *Prime 100: Writing Reports That Work*. rev ed. New York: AMACOM, 1980. One volume looseleaf.

Learning report writing is accomplished with a programmed study guide. The manual, handbook, programmed course and text booklet fit into one three-ring binder. The handbook discloses the basics of creating reports and examples of a letter of transmittal, outline, abstract and summary. It refers to the programmed instruction book for the seven sections of writing skills in a workbook format. A glossary is in most sections. Not indexed.

RESUMES

806. Allen, Jeffrey G. *The Complete Q and A Job Interview Book*. New York: John Wiley and Sons, 1988. 213p.

The author, a placement attorney, offers training in answering interview questions. The hundreds of commonly-asked questions are tied to sections of a resume or job application, i.e. education background and work experience. This volume is useful for both interviewer and interviewee. Indexed.

807. Angel, J. L. *Effective Resumes for Executives and Specialized Personnel.* 2d ed. New York: Monarch Press, 1980. 184p.

The book concentrates on self-marketing techniques and resume preparation for managerial and technical professionals. The numerous model resumes are arranged by kind of position with an index. Cover letters with samples appear in chapter eight. Indexed.

808. Antinozzi, M. A. *The Practical Resume: A Writer's Guide.* Westport, CT: Writers Workshop, 1983. 160p.

This approach to creating a resume, for both beginners and more experienced workers, uses the viewpoint of those who read the resumes. There are seventy-five samples with an index. Indexed.

809. Armstrong, Fiona; Baum, Myra K.; and Miller, Joan B. *A Realistic Job Search.* New York: McGraw-Hill, 1980. 168p.

Elementary guidance is advanced on the employment search in a workbook. The pretest and exercises instruct students about resumes, cover letters, employment tests and interviews. The book has some self-evaluation tests, sample cover letters, and answers for the exercises. Not indexed.

810. Aulick, June L., ed. *Resumes for Employment in the U.S. and Overseas.* 3d ed. New York:World Trade Academy Press, 1988. 125p.

Volume unavailable for examination.

811. Beatty, Richard H. *The Complete Job Search Book.* New York: John Wiley and Sons, 1988. 244p.

There are five chapters on resumes in this how-to job hunting book. The author explores good and bad resumes, the characteristics of chronological and functional resumes, and the preparation stages with blank forms. All five chapters have sample resumes. Indexed.

812. Beatty, Richard H. *The Resume Kit.* New York: John Wiley and Sons, 1984. 265p.

Based on the author's experience as a personnel executive, the book discusses resume myths and competition strategies. The practical guidance is accompanied by samples of chronological, functional resumes and cover letters. There are some blank worksheets. Indexed.

813. Biegeleisen, J. I. *How to Write Your First Professional Resume.* New York: Perigee Books, Putnam Publishing, 1986. 112p.

As a basic introduction for beginners to writing a resume and cover letter, the volume reveals model resumes, cover letters and thank you letters. A form for a self-appraisal personality rating scale is in the appendices. Blank worksheets are available. Indexed.

814. Bisdee, Bob. *Steer Your Own Career. A Practical Guide to Effective and Satisfying Career Change.* New York: Nichols Publishing, 1988. 174p.

The author concentrates on guidance for the employment search or a career change. The blank evaluation forms for goals and skills includes an extensive job skills grid. Chapter eight discloses different types of resumes with model documents. Not indexed.

815. Bostwick, Burdette E. *Resume Writing. A Comprehensive How-to-do-it Guide*. 3d ed. New York: John Wiley and Sons, 1985. 323p.

The book is designed to produce a sophisticated tool for marketing oneself. Chapter eleven investigates ten resume styles with explanation and samples. Additional samples are in Appendix A and can be located through the subject index. The appendices provide useful words and phrases, job responsibilities by classification and hiring statistics. Indexed.

816. Brennan, Lawrence D.; Strand, Stanley; and Gruber, Edward C. *Resumes for Better Jobs*. New York: Arco Publishing, Prentice-Hall, 1987. 202p.

The collection of numerous business-oriented resumes is followed by advice on writing resumes and cover letters. All models are structured according to the guidelines presented. A separate alphabetical list of occupations appears early in the book. Indexed.

817. Calhoun, Mary E. *How to Get the Hot Jobs in Business and Finance*. New York: Harper and Row, 1985. 191p.

A revised edition of the author's previous book, this guide to achieving a wall street career focuses on career choices. Different financial careers and the job hunting process are described. Chapter three presents guidelines and samples for the resume and cover letter. Part four lists resource directories and five hundred financial firms. Not indexed.

818. Corwen, Leonard. *Your Resume: Key to a Better Job*. 3d ed. New York: Arco Publishing, 1988. 176p.

This revision is much improved over the second edition. In part one resumes are created with blank worksheets for the personal assessment inventory. There are sample resumes and cover letters. There is an index of resume job titles. Part two addresses aspects of the employment process. The appendices include information sources, job-search control sheet and further reading. Some sample resumes in the second edition list personal data (age, marital status) that is no longer required or recommended. Indexed.

819. Cowan, Tom. *Resumes That Work*. New York; Scarborough, Canada: New American Library, 1983. 177p.

Three resume types are examined with models: skill-based, chronological and functional. There are blank qualifications worksheets and an index by field. The discussion of cover letters features eleven samples. Caution should be exercised as some resume samples include personal data. While the text follows current federal regulations, inclusion of personal data is recommended by the author under some circumstances. Indexed.

820. Coxford, Lola M. *Resume Writing Made Easy for High Tech*. Scottsdale, AZ: Gorsuch Scarisbrick, 1987. 143p.

The job search and writing techniques here stress high technology positions. The numerous sample resumes are arranged according to career stages: entry level, transition and moving up. There is a separate alphabetical index to the sample resumes. Blank forms for a personal inventory and a personal review are available. Indexed.

821. Croft, Barbara L. *Getting a Job: Resume Writing, Job Application Letters, and Interview Strategies*. Columbus, OH: Merrill Publishing Company, 1989. 143p.
Volume unavailable for examination.

822. Dawson, Kenneth M. *Job Search: The Total System*. John Wiley and Sons, 1988. 244p.
The job search manual was prepared by two downsizing specialists. Techniques and advice are given for an active employment search using such methods as telemarketing, networking and others. Chapter three shows the resume, with sample resumes in the appendix. Indexed.

823. Dickhut, Harold W. *The Executive Resume Handbook*. New York: Prentice-Hall, 1987. 215p.
Designed for the executive level job search or job change, resumes and cover letters are investigated. The author provides guidelines, instructions and numerous samples. Indexed.

824. Dickhut, Harold W. *The Professional Resume and Job Search Guide*. Englewood Cliffs, NJ: Prentice-Hall, 1981. 218p.
Sections two through eight lead step-by-step through the process of creating an effective resume with models. The remainder of the book presents job search strategies, cover letters and job interviews. Indexed.

825. Faux, Marian. *Clear and Simple Guide to Resume Writing*. Abr ed. New York: Monarch Press, 1980. 135p.
This is a basic guide to development of the resume and cover letter. An abridged edition of the complete guide, the book displays a resume checklist, blank worksheets and numerous model resumes. Not indexed.

826. Faux, Marian. *The Complete Resume Guide*. 2d ed. New York: Monarch Press, 1980. 184p.
The many sample resumes and index are in chapter three. The book addresses the concerns of the over forty and the disabled worker. Indexed.

827. Faux, Marian. *Entering the Job Market. A College Graduate's Guide to Job Hunting*. New York: Monarch Press, 1984. 153p.
The author's job hunting method emphasizes special techniques for new graduates and for the tight job market. Chapter four considers cover letters, chapter five, the resume and samples. In the author's other books the resume is analyzed better. Not indexed.

828. Feld, Warren S. *How High Can You Fly*. New York: Prentice-Hall, 1986. 248p.
The resume and career guide offers career guidance for professionals with experience and/or graduate education. Resumes, cover letters, business cards

and career strategies such as joining professional groups are related. There are sample resumes and a career choice worksheet. Not indexed.

829. Fox, Marcia R. *Put Your Degree to Work. The New Professional's Guide to Career Planning and Job Hunting*. 2d ed. New York: W. W. Norton and Company, 1988. 251p.

The job search process described here points up the importance of networking and other techniques. The chapters on resumes and cover letters include samples and a cover-letter checklist. Indexed.

830. Foxman, L. D. *The Key to Your Successful Resume: How to Sell Yourself on Paper*. Chicago: L. D. Foxman, Cambridge Human Resource Group, 1982. 96p.

Concise directions on writing resumes and cover letters appear in a workbook with models. There are blank worksheets for skills inventory, resume preparation and the job search stages. Not indexed.

831. Fry, Ronald W. *Your First Resume: The Comprehensive Preparation Guide for High School and College Students*. Hawthorne, NJ: Career Press, 1988. 156p.

Volume unavailable for examination.

832. Gerberg, Robert J. *Robert Gerberg's Job Changing System*. Kansas City, MO: Andrews, McMeel and Parker, 1984. 265p.

The author proposes a specific system for moving up in a field or changing career fields. While stressing professional and managerial levels, the book explains how to create outstanding resumes and letters. There are numerous examples, a blank resume questionnaire, a financial planning guide and plan-of-action forms. Indexed.

833. Gray, Ernest A. *Successful Business Resumes*. Boston: CBI Publishing Company, 1981. 285p.

There are eleven steps in forming a successful resume. The sample resumes illustrate particular situations as defined in the case studies. Part three is a workbook containing instructions and eleven forms for resume preparation. Not indexed.

834. Healey, Mary. *The Job-Winning Resume Kit*. Westbury, NY: Caddylak Publishing, 1985. 129p.

Volume unavailable for examination.

835. Hizer, David V., and Rosenberg, Arthur D. *Paper Tiger: Resume Strategies That Get Your Foot in the Door*. Boston: Bob Adams, 1985. 136p.

A resume can be built with these techniques and principles. The book focuses on organization, basic principles, and the use of action-oriented language. There are models of the best and worst resumes. Not indexed.

836. Holtz, Herman. *Beyond the Resume*. New York: McGraw-Hill, 1984. 234p.

Job hunting and resume preparation are offered as elements of a sales transaction, with examples. The author suggests ways to improve the outcome and introduces the super resume with models. Indexed.

837. Jackson, Tom. *The Perfect Resume*. Garden City: Anchor Books, 1981. 208p.

Volume unavailable for examination.

838. King, James B. *Negotiating the Brier Patch: Resume and Job Search Strategies for the College Senior*. Dubuque, IA: Kendall/Hunt Publishing, 1986. 136p.

A guide to locating that first job, the book has suggestions and techniques for the search and for resume preparation. There are several model resumes. Not indexed.

839. Kisiel, Marie. *Design for Change: A Guide to New Careers*. New York: New Viewpoints, 1980. 334p.

A plan or series of steps are furnished for changing careers. Three kinds of resumes are shown with examples and blank personal inventory sheets. The appendix lists sources of additional information. Indexed.

840. Komar, John J. *The Resume Builder*. Piscataway, NJ: New Century Publishers, 1980. 119p.

The author identifies nine steps to a powerful resume, design of an application letter, and solutions for qualification problems. Sample resumes appear in the appendix. Not indexed.

841. Krannich, Ronald L., and Banis, William J. *High Impact Resumes and Letters*. Manassas, VA: Impact Publications, 1982. 134p.

A self-directed format is used to present the job search process. Basic concepts, production techniques, and marketing strategies are unveiled. Useful blank forms appear in the text, with sample letters and resumes in the appendices. A new edition is scheduled for 1988. Indexed.

842. Lewis, Adele. *Better Resumes for College Graduates*. Woodbury, NY: Barron's Educational Series, 1985. 154p.

Presented here are guidelines for creating a resume and conducting a job search. The author advances concise descriptions, model resumes and worksheet forms. Not indexed.

843. Lewis, Adele. *Better Resumes for Sales and Marketing Personnel*. Woodbury, NY: Barron's Educational Series, 1985. 236p.

This job-hunting guide is aimed at sales and marketing personnel. The book contains production steps for resumes and cover letters. There are blank resume worksheets and many sample resumes. Indexed.

844. Lewis, Adele. *How to Write Better Resumes*. 2d ed. Woodbury, NY: Barron's Educational Series, 1983. 298p.

This volume, in designing the resume, concentrates on writing skills. The text relates several approaches and a large number of model resumes. Job descriptions are in the appendix. There is an index to model resumes. Indexed.

845. Lewis, Adele, and Hartman, Berl. *Better Resumes for Computer Personnel*. Woodbury, NY: Barron's Educational Series, 1984. 220p.

The resume is stressed as part of the job search process for computer professionals. There are guidelines, checklists, blank worksheets and numerous sample resumes. Models are grouped into six categories of computer professionals. Not indexed.

846. Lewis, William. *Resumes for College Graduates*. rev ed. New York: Monarch Press, 1984. 95p.

Volume unavailable for examination.

847. Lico, Laurie E. *Resumes for Executive Women: Strategic Approaches for the Upwardly-Mobile Career Woman*. New York: Simon and Schuster, 1984. 128p.

Volume unavailable for examination.

848. Lico, Laurie E. *Resumes for Successful Women*. New York: Wallaby Book, Pocket Books, 1985. 125p.

Based on interviews with professionals, the author discloses guidelines for successful resumes in a volume designed for women. The elements of resume writing, blank worksheets, and sample resumes apply to any situation. There are bibliographies of books and resource material in the appendices. Not indexed.

849. Linkemer, Bobbi. *How to Write an Effective Resume*. New York: AMACOM, 1987. 58p.

The small, pamphlet-sized book gives practical suggestions and strategies for resumes. There are model resumes in the appendix. Not indexed.

850. Lock, Robert D. *Job Search*. Pacific Grove, CA: Brooks/Cole Publishing, 1988. 248p.

Conducting a job search is approached by the author in several ways. Chapter three conveys techniques for resume writing with sample documents and blank worksheets. Indexed.

851. McLaughlin, John E., and Merman, Stephen K. *Writing a Job-Winning Resume*. Englewood Cliffs, NJ: Prentice-Hall, 1980. 180p.

Instructions are provided for different types of resumes. The author stresses development of a resume in one evening. Besides the how-to advice there are twenty case studies (in chapter ten), examples and model resumes. Uncovering job leads is handled in a section on letters. Indexed.

852. Males, Carolyn, and Feigen, Roberta. *Life After High School. A Career Planning Guide*. New York: Julian Messner, 1986. 163p.

In a career guide for high school graduates, chapter six briefly examines the different kinds of resumes with examples. The book is not as useful for more advanced workers. Indexed.

853. *Marketing Yourself. The Catalyst Women's guide to Successful Resumes and Interviews*. By The Catalyst Staff. New York: G. P. Putnam's Sons, 1980. 185p.

The Catalyst has combined its previously published book on resumes with guidelines for interviewing. There are clear instructions, examples and blank worksheets. Not indexed.

854. Mazzo, Karen E. *How to Write Your Own Professional Resume. A Step-By-Step Guide on Writing Your Own Professional Resume.* Glenmont, NY: DTM Associates, 1980. 44p.

Based on the author's experience in running a resume service, this booklet proceeds step-by-step to construct a professional resume. The process is explained with examples of each section of the resume. The author has included personal data in the examples which is no longer required or recommended. The exhibits contain sample resumes (in different formats) and blank worksheets (for the rough draft). Not indexed.

855. Nadler, Burton J. *Liberal Arts Power.* Princeton, NJ: Peterson's Guides, 1985. 118p.

Liberal arts graduates can find job search guidelines and resume advice in this work. There are numerous sample resumes, each with an accompanying analysis. The author also supplies cover letters, sample skills chart and employment target chart. Not indexed.

856. Parker, Yana. *The Damn Good Resume Guide.* Berkeley, CA: Ten Speed Press, 1983. 60p.

Blank skill assessment forms, models and guidelines are used by the author to fashion resumes. The appendices show action verbs, questions and employer critiques of resumes. Not indexed.

857. Parker, Yana. *The Resume Catalog: 200 Damn Good Examples.* Berkeley, CA: Ten Speed Press, 1988. 314p.

Volume unavailable for examination.

858. Payne, Richard A. *How to Get a Better Job Quicker.* 3d ed. New York: Taplinger Publishing Company, 1987. 242p.

The plans and techniques in this volume support the search for a job. Search strategies and interviewing are stressed. There are no sample resumes. Not indexed.

859. Pell, Arthur R., and Sadek, George. *Resumes for Computer Professionals.* New York: Monarch Press, 1984. 111p.

Designed for computer professionals, the authors explain career choices, resume design and the different formats. A preparation inventory and blank worksheets are available along with thirty sample resumes. The models demonstrate the inclusion of foreign languages, personal computing skills and security clearances. Not indexed.

860. Pell, Arthur R., and Sadek, George. *Resumes for Engineers.* New York: Monarch Press, 1982. 118p.

Volume unavailable for examination.

861. Perlmutter, Deborah E. *How to Write a Winning Resume*. Lincolnwood, IL: VGM Career Horizons, National Textbook Company, 1985. 117p.

Based in part on a survey of employer's expectations, the author directs readers through the resume process. There are samples of resumes. Other sources of information and one hundred job descriptions appear in the appendices. Not indexed.

862. *Putting It in Writing*. Frankfort, KY: Education Associates, 1984. 16p.

Volume unavailable for examination.

863. *Resumes That Get Jobs*. 4th ed. Edited by Jean Reed. New York: Arco Publishing, Prentice-Hall, 1986. 178p.

Primarily a collection of model resumes, this book briefly considers resume content and it's use in a job search. There is a separate subject index to the model resumes. Indexed.

864. Rogers, Edward J. *Getting Hired. Everything You Need to Know About Resumes, Interviews, and Job-Hunting Strategies*. Englewood Cliffs, NJ: Prentice-Hall, 1982. 196p.

Amidst the job hunting guidelines and techniques, the basic resume is formed with illustrative samples. Designed as a resource book, related sources are listed in the appendices. The text recommends the inclusion of three to eight personal interest items on the resume. Some models state date of birth in this category. Indexed.

865. Schuman, Nancy and Lewis, William. *Revising Your Resume*. New York: John Wiley and Sons, 1986. 156p.

The common-sense approach advances sixty rules for improving a resume. There are seventeen sample resumes, a checklist and blank worksheets. Indexed.

866. Shanahan, William F. *Resumes for Computer Professionals*. New York: Arco Publishing, 1983. 123p.

For computer professionals, there is advice and guidelines for the job search and the resume. Different kinds of resumes are shown with numerous models, a blank personal information sheet, and resume index. Indexed.

867. Shanahan, William. *Resumes for Engineers*. New York: Arco Publishing, 1983. 129p.

Volume unavailable for examination.

868. Shykind, Maury. *Resumes for Executives and Professionals*. 3d ed. New York: Arco Publishing, 1984. 199p.

The author reviews the development and implementation of a marketing plan for executives. Clear steps for the resume are related, with blank self-assessment forms and numerous models. Not indexed.

869. Smith, Michael H. *The Resume Writer's Handbook*. 2d ed. New York: Barnes and Noble, 1987. 184p.

The many facets of resume writing are examined with fifty sample resumes. Separate sections contain the solutions for common problems and address related letter-writing techniques. Blank worksheets appear in the appendix. Not indexed.

870. Summers, Jean. *What Every Woman Needs to Know to Find a Job in Today's Tough Market*. New York: Fawcett Columbine, 1980. 191p.

Tips and strategies are furnished for women who are looking for employment. The resume and cover letter models show how the guidelines are implemented. The book contains a skills inventory and exercises. Not indexed.

871. Turbak, Gary. *Action-Getting Resumes for Today's Jobs*. New York: Arco Publishing, 1983. 166p.

This book describes what a resume is and how to construct one. Three resume formats, the cover letter and the interview are discussed. The sixty sample resumes are indexed by occupation. Indexed.

872. Ulrich, Heinz. *How to Prepare Your Own High-Intensity Resume*. rev ed. Englewood Cliffs, NJ: Prentice-Hall, 1983. 216p.

The author offers guidelines, worksheets and models for building a resume and cover letter. The job-hunting gameplan employs a workbook arrangement. Not indexed.

873. Washington, Tom. *Resume Power: Selling Yourself on Paper*. Bellevue, WA: Mount Vernon Press, 1988. 288p.

All phases of the job search process are anticipated. A quality resume can be fashioned with the practical guidelines and techniques. The book focuses separately on each element of the resume. There are over seventy sample resumes and cover letters listed alphabetically by subject. The 1988 edition contains basically the same content as the 1985 edition. Not indexed.

874. Wegmann, Robert, and Chapman, Robert. *The Right Place at the Right Time. Finding a Job in the New Economy*. Berkeley, CA: Ten Speed Press, 1987. 211p.

This book is a handy introduction to the job search process. Designed as a textbook, it provides useful exercises and blank worksheets for both a skills inventory and a personality analysis. The appendix to chapter eight considers resume preparation with models. Based on the author's previous book on finding employment in Houston, it has one of the best sections on reseearching an industry and an occupation. Indexed.

875. Weinstein, Bob. *Resumes for Hard Times*. New York: Fireside Book, Simon and Schuster, 1982. 127p.

Stages for resume creation are shown as part of the job search process. For the resume there are sample documents and a checklist. The blank forms are for the self-evaluation test, the resume (worksheets) and the skills inventory (chart). Not indexed.

876. Wilson, Robert. *Resumes for Executives and Professionals*. Woodbury, NY: Barron's, 1983. 259p.

Volume unavailable for examination.

SUMMARIES

877. Keene, Michael L. *Effective Professional Writing*. Lexington, MA: D. C. Heath, 1987. 450p.

The professional writing textbook is for technical and business students. It highlights written communication, with coverage of abstracts and summaries, letters, proposals and reports. There are many examples and a sample long report. Indexed.

878. Laster, Ann A., and Pickett, Nell A. *Occupational English*. 3d ed. New York: Harper and Row, 1981. 449p.

For students in an occupational education program, the textbook is a practical writing guide. The authors combine the principles and forms of writing with practice and samples of summaries, letters and reports. There are blank planning sheets for each type of writing discussed. Oral communication, grammar and usage are briefly reported. Indexed.

879. Paxson, William C. *The Business Writing Handbook*. Toronto: Bantam Books, 1981. 274p.

The essentials of organizing and writing are practiced with examples and model letters, memos, proposals and reports. Part three consists of a grammar review, part four of an editing guide. Indexed.

Chapter 6

ORAL COMMUNICATION

Communicating on the job requires the ability to converse with colleagues, management and customers in a variety of situations. Working with others means face-to-face communication for different reasons. The good communicator speaks and listens, and can communicate by telephone, with the media, and on television.

This chapter concerns the acquisition and development of specific oral skills and their application to employment situations. The two most important skills are speaking and listening. Effective customer service requires responsive listening and persuasive speaking. Used daily in every conversation, the level of skill demanded is high for those participating in personnel interactions, formal presentations, and interviews.

Interviewing skills are needed for hiring new employees, evaluating current ones, and communicating with all of them. Uncertainties about an interview's structure, the questions permitted and legal limits are handled by the books in this chapter.

Meetings are a fact of life. They occur for many reasons and in various sized groups. Both leaders and participants can guarantee the success of a meeting. Corporate training conjures up visions of workshops and seminars. The skills needed for planning and conducting these sessions transfer, on a larger scale, to ensuring productive conferences and conventions.

Formal presentations, speeches and oral reports are delivered at conferences and meetings. New procedures, products and processes are presented internally to corporate groups or externally to clients and colleagues. Many practitioners have published suggestions for mastering oral communication skills. Presentations, speeches and reports can be created easily with the outlines, techniques, methods, and samples in this chapter.

Managers and executives occasionally are placed in situations affecting public opinion and having wide-ranging consequences for the company. When a thoughtful response is demanded, today's executive needs skills in media relations, using the telephone, handling question and answer sessions and being interviewed on television. Some are called to represent their organization in an official capacity as an expert witness. This chapter offers techniques, guidelines and models for the development or improvement of these skills.

CONFERENCES AND CONVENTIONS

880. Carnes, William T. *Effective Meetings for Busy People. Let's Decide It and Go Home*. New York: The Institute of Electrical and Electronics Engineers, 1987. 348p.

The author has reissued his 1980 book with an additional preface commenting on the continuing validity of his work. The book presents an approach to the organization and control of meetings, conferences and seminars called the Goldfish Bowl Technique. This method promotes parallel decision making and can be used by attendees as well as conference organizers . There are additional chapters on running committees and preparing the committee report. Indexed.

881. Jeffries, James R., and Bates, Jefferson D. *The Executive's Guide to Meetings, Conferences, and Audiovisual Presentations*. New York: McGraw-Hill, 1983. 226p.

Insights are given for the organization, preparation and management of group meetings, conferences and seminars with illustrations. The book emphasizes the choice, use and preparation of audiovisual materials in creating a presentation. The tips can be applied to situations other than business. There is a glossary of audiovisual terms. Indexed.

882. Lord, Robert W. *Running Conventions, Conferences, and Meetings*. New York: AMACOM, 1981. 192p.

Practical guidelines are disclosed for planning and conducting conventions, workshops and similar meetings. The book stresses conventions with examples. Indexed.

EXPERT TESTIMONY

883. Casagrande, Diane O., and Casagrande, Roger D. *Oral Communication in Technical Professions and Business*. Belmont, CA: Wadsworth Publishing Company, 1986. 354p.

Designed as a textbook for technical students, the authors offer guidance for professionals in chapters ten through fourteen. Many examples illustrate the discussions of meetings, interviewing, presentations, and expert testimony. A glossary of related terminology is included. Indexed.

INTERVIEWING

884. Adler, Ronald B. *Communicating at Work*. 2d ed. New York: Random House, 1986. 387p.

This volume surveys survival skills such as: personal skills, group communication and presentations. Practical information is given on meetings, interviews and presentations. The well-footnoted chapters have many examples and an activities section. Indexed.

885. Beatty, Richard H. *The Five Minute Interview*. New York: John Wiley and Sons, 1986. 201p.

For the person being interviewed, the author presents the five minute interview, a how-to approach. Stressing the development of a strategic approach, the interview focuses on the goals of the institution. The five minute interview consists of questions to be asked by the candidate during the first minutes of an interview. There are exercises and over four hundred commonly-asked questions. Indexed.

886. Bell, Arthur H. *The Complete Manager's Guide to Interviewing: How to Hire the Best*. Homewood, IL: Dow Jones-Irwin, 1989. 214p.

For managers, this manual relates interviewing techniques. The author's interview blueprint (in chapter seven) outlines the steps necessary for any interview. The guide offers checklists and sample questions. In the appendix, the handbook examines different types of interviews. There are sample questions and forms. Indexed.

887. Bolton, G. M. *Interviewing for Selection Decisions*. Windsor, Berkshire, UK: NFER-Nelson Publishing Company, 1983. 31p.

This is a brief look at employment interviewing. Based partially on research conducted by the National Institute of Industrial Psychology and by Edward Webster, the interview process is examined in chronological order. There are guidelines, rating scales and other suggestions. Not indexed.

888. Donaghy, William C. *The Interview: Skills and Applications*. Glenview, IL: Scott Foresman, 1984. 436p.

In this textbook, eight basic interviewing skills are described in ten interview situations. Sample forms and interview questions are in the chapters on specific interviews. There is an extensive bibliography of related books and periodicals. Indexed.

889. Downs, Cal W.; Smeyak, G. Paul; and Martin, Ernest. *Professional Interviewing*. New York: Harper and Row, 1980. 432p.

Directed at professionals and students, skill development is accomplished through a cafeteria approach to interviewing. Part two, on management related interviews, deals with selection, appraisal, discipline and exit interviews. There are guidelines and examples. Indexed.

890. Drake, John D. *Effective Interviewing: A Guide for Managers*. New York: AMACOM, 1982. 275p.

This is basically the same book as the revised edition of *Interviewing for Managers*. Indexed.

891. Drake, John D. *Interviewing for Managers*. rev ed. New York: AMACOM, 1982. 275p.

Managers are shown the hypothesis method (chapter seven) for evaluating job candidates. The how-to book emphasizes the conduct and structure of interviews through self-appraisal questions. The self-appraisal questions are listed in chapter nine. Sample questions, forms and checklists appear in the appendix. Indexed.

892. Einhorn, Lois J.; Bradley, Patricia H.; and Baird, John E. Jr. *Effective Employment Interviewing*. Glenview, IL: Scott Foresman, 1982. 164p.

The employment interview is examined from the perspective of both applicant and employer. Fundamental communication principles are considered and applied to the interview. The authors provide sample questions, letters and resumes. Indexed.

893. Evans, David R. et al. *Essential Interviewing: A Programmed Approach to Effective Communication*. 2d ed. Monterey, CA: Brooks/Cole Publishing Company, 1984. 209p.

A systematic approach to interviewing skills is implemented in a programmed text. For eight basic skill areas, are specific formulas and methods. Based partially on the micro-counseling concept of single skills, the authors are concerned primarily with counseling interviews. Some portions can be used to enhance personnel decision skills, particularly chapter five on listening and chapter nine on confronting skills. The third edition should become available in 1988. Indexed.

894. Fear, Richard A. *The Evaluation Interview*. 3d ed. New York: McGraw-Hill, 1984. 330p.

For managers, there are instructions on hiring qualified people at all levels. The entire process is considered, from gathering information, to evaluating data and preparing the final report. The interview rating guide, form and sample reports are in the appendices. Indexed.

895. Goodale, James G. *The Fine Art of Interviewing*. Englewood Cliffs, NJ: Prentice-Hall, 1982. 201p.

The principles of planning and conducting six business interviews, from election to exit ones, are examined. The approach and guidelines are highlighted rather than key questions. Indexed.

896. Goodworth, Clive T. *Effective Interviewing for Employment Selection*. rev ed. London: Business Books, 1983. 138p.

Designed for British companies, the author stresses the need for learning how to interview. Examples and self-tutorials are used for hiring clerical or support personnel. The sample questions on personal and family matters are inappropriate in the United States. Indexed.

897. Gratus, Jack. *Successful Interviewing: How to Find and Keep the Best People*. New York: Viking Penguin, 1988. 93p.

Volume unavailable for examination.

898. Hamilton, Cheryl, and Parker, Cordell. *Communicating for Results*. 2d ed. Belmont, CA: Wadsworth Publishing Company, 1987. 418p.

The authors review interpersonal and organizational communication skills with pertinent examples. Among the skill areas reported are interviewing, listening and oral presentations. The sample interview questions, which have been reprinted from other sources, appear in appendices B and C. Indexed.

899. Hanna, Michael S., and Wilson, Gerald L. *Communicating in Business and Professional Settings*. 2d ed. New York: Random House, 1988. 445p.

The organizational communications textbook combines theory and application in considering selection interviews, appraisal interviews, reports, proposals, meetings and presentations. The book contains sample interview questions, resumes, a conference planning checklist and an outline of a speech. The text has an unusual problem-solution index that directs students to the pages where problems are addressed. Indexed.

900. Hodgson, Philip. *A Practical Guide to Successful Interviewing*. London: McGraw-Hill, 1987. 94p.

Interviewing techniques are disclosed for busy managers. Each interview is investigated with a checklist, examples and questions. Indexed.

901. Hopper, Robert. *Between You and Me*. In consultation with Lillian J. Davis. Glenview, IL: Scott Foresman, 1984. 144p.

Six skills for effective interpersonal communication are reviewed. This method covers listening, interviews and group interactions in a business context with examples and checklists. Indexed.

902. *How to Conduct Lawful and Effective Interviews*. 2d ed. New York: John Wiley and Sons, 1984. 143p.

The workbook, with accompanying cassettes, reviews interviewing approaches and techniques for managers. The a self-teaching workbook offers sample interviews and related documents. Not indexed.

903. Hunt, Gary T., and Eadie, William F. *Interviewing. A Communications Approach*. New York: Holt, Rinehart and Winston, 1987. 247p.

Five basic communication skills are applied to different kinds of interviews. Useful for both participants and interviewer, the book has guidelines, special issues, problems and many sample interviews. Indexed.

904. Janz, Tom; Hellervik, Lowell; and Gilmore, David C. *Behavior Description Interviewing*. Boston: Allyn and Bacon, 1986. 249p.

A specific interviewing method for hiring decisions is described. Self-test questions can be found in each chapter. The sample interview questions in Appendix A are arranged by type of position. Use of the samples requires an understanding of question design and results evaluation. Indexed.

905. McQuaig, Jack H.; McQuaig, Peter L.; and McQuaig, Donald H. *How to Interview and Hire Productive People*. New York: Frederick Fell Publishers, 1981. 303p.

Based on the author's 1963 work, managers are supplied with selection interview guidelines. There are sample questions and a typical interview in the appendices. Not indexed.

906. Molyneaux, Dorothy, and Lane, Vera W. *Effective Interviewing: Techniques and Analysis*. Boston: Allyn and Bacon, 1982. 244p.

For students and experienced professionals, the authors reveal their method for analyzing interviews. Chapters 5-8 discuss preparing for and conducting the interview. Specific types of interviews are not delineated. The appendices include an analysis form and the authors'research results. Indexed.

907. Morgan, Henry H., and Cogger, John W. *The Interviewer's Manual.* 2d ed. New York: Drake Beam Morin, 1980. 117p.

The principles and techniques here focus on the selection or evaluation interview. They can be applied to other types of interviews and meetings. Writing the final report is handled as well. Sample forms appear in the appendix. Not indexed.

908. Olson, Richard F. *Managing the Interview.* New York: John Wiley and Sons, 1980. 183p.

While summarizing research on interviewing, this concise book advances suggestions, guidelines, do's and don'ts for managers. The goal is to change a manager's approach to interviewing. This self-help book promotes skill development with application and review questions and answers. After consideration of an interview's parts, the strategies are presented. Indexed.

909. Pearce, C. Glenn; Figgins, Ross; and Golen, Steven P. *Business Communication: Principles and Applications.* 2d ed. New York: John Wiley and Sons, 1988. 745p.

The business communication textbook combines communication theory and skill development for letters, memos, reports, proposals, presentations, listening, interviewing and meetings. This is one of the few textbooks which reviews interviewing skills. The book displays examples in draft and revised format. There are models of letters, resumes and parts of a reports. Grammar assistance and business research sources can be found in the appendices. Indexed.

910. Phillips, Gerald M. *Communicating in Organizations.* New York: Macmillan, 1982. 366p.

The author conveys instructions for communicating in organizations. There are realistic guidelines for interviewing, presentations and basic written documents. A model simulation appears in the appendix. Indexed.

911. Rae, Leslie. *The Skills of Interviewing. A Guide for Managers and Trainers.* New York: Nichols Publishing Company, 1988. 212p.

The author's interview strategies reinforce the importance of listening and question development. Designed for managers, five kinds of interviews are investigated as to objectives, preparation, structure and behavior. This book can be used as a self-instructional guide. Indexed.

912. Ramsay, Roland T. *Management's Guide to Effective Employment Interviewing. Tested Techniques of Personnel Selection.* Chicago: Dartnell Corporation, 1980. 315p.

Psychological research and personnel procedures are employed in interviewing. The author's plan uses guidelines, checklists, sample forms and sample questions in featuring employment and supervising interviews. Pertinent rules and regulations are in the appendices. Indexed.

913. Rosenblatt, S. Bernard; Cheatham, T. Richard; and Watt, James T. *Communication in Business.* 2d ed. Englewood Cliffs, NJ: Prentice-Hall, 1982. 404p.

This introductory survey textbook sponsors interviewing, presentations, letters and reports through a systems approach. There are many examples. Indexed.

914. Samovar, Larry A., and Hellweg, Susan A. *Interviewing: A Communicative Approach.* Dubuque, IA: Gorsuch Scarishrick Publishers, 1982. 54p.

Advice is offered for improving one's performance in selection, evaluation and persuasive interviews. The book has study questions and activities. Four evaluation forms are in the appendix. Indexed.

915. Schroeer, Susan G. *Successful Hiring Through Skillful Interviewing Techniques.* Westbury, NY: Asher-Gallant Press, 1988. 000p. (Pagination unavailable)

Volume unavailable for examination.

916. Sincoff, Michael Z., and Goyer, Robert S. *Interviewing.* New York: Macmillan Publishing Company; London: Collier Macmillan, 1984. 273p.

Informational, survey, persuasive, employment, appraisal and exit interviews are shown. The text considers pitfalls, typical questions, checklists and sample forms. Indexed.

917. Smart, Bradford D. *Selection Interviewing: A Management Psychologist's Recommended Approach.* New York: John Wiley and Sons, 1983. 292p.

Selection interviews are conducted using a specific method. There are principles, recommended steps and guidelines. Sample forms and questions are in the appendices. Indexed.

918. Stano, Michael E., and Reinsch, N. L. Jr. *Communication in Interviews.* Englewood Cliffs, NJ: Prentice-Hall, 1982. 233p.

Interviewing is viewed as the application of interpersonal communication skills. This scholarly approach focuses on nine interviews as variations on accepted interviewing principles and practices. Indexed.

919. Stewart, Charles J., and Cash, William B. Jr. *Interviewing Principles and Practices.* 5th ed. Dubuque, IA: Wm. C. Brown, 1988. 283p.

Techniques for use in seven interviewing situations are examined. This edition reflects current research and equal opportunity legislation. The chapter on the selection interview includes a model of the resume. Indexed.

920. Swan, William S. *Swan's How to Pick the Right People Program.* Written with Phillip Margulis, Maxine Rosaler and Hillary S. Kayle. New York: John Wiley and Sons, 1989. 284p.

Developed from the author's many seminars on selection interviewing, the book describes an interview plan. Managers are introduced to question formulation, data gathering and organization and decision making. The last section of the volume shows how to fit this interview method into a corporate hiring system. Indexed.

921. Uris, Auren. *88 Mistakes Interviewers Make -- And How to Avoid Them.* New York: American Management Association, 1988. 252p.

The author offers solutions for over eighty common interview errors. Based partly on survey results, the underscores the importance of prevention through the identification of specific problem situations. Each unit introduces a mistake, gives an example, and proscribes corrective behavior. Indexed.

922. Weiss, Donald H. *How to Be a Successful Interviewer.* New York: American Management Association, 1988. 58p.

The small pocketbook presents the design of job descriptions and the four stages of the initial interview. Position specifications are shown in Figure 3. There are blank worksheets for a task analysis in the appendix. Indexed.

923. Zima, Joseph P. *Interviewing: Key to Effective Management.* Chicago: Science Research Associates, 1983. 436p.

This very thorough volume considers interviewing in eleven different situations. For each interview there are objectives, checklists, examples, openings, closings, sample questions and forms. Permissible areas for discussion are disclosed for the employment interview. There are role-playing exercises and cases. Indexed.

LISTENING

924. Anastasi, Thomas E. Jr. *Listen! Techniques for Improving Communication Skills.* Boston: CBI Publishing Company, 1982. 99p.

The self-training guide sponsors listening skill improvement. Adapted from the author's earlier work, *Face-to-Face Communication*, this brief volume contains steps, guidelines and listening techniques for meetings, interviews and presentations. An index would greatly improve the effectiveness of this volume. Not indexed.

925. Brownell, Judi. *Building Active Listening Skills.* Englewood Cliffs, NJ: Prentice-Hall, 1986. 314p.

The how-to approach fosters development and improvement of listening skills. The format and questionnaire in chapter one encourages use of the book as a self-paced guide. Chapter eight relates listening in specific situations such as listening to subordinates. Indexed.

926. Burley-Allen, Madelyn. *Listening: The Forgotten Skill.* New York: John Wiley and Sons, 1982. 153p.

Listening skills are shown to enhance professional and personal growth. Not related specifically to the business arena, the guidelines, techniques and exercises pertain to all situations. Indexed.

927. Glatthorn, Allan A., and Adams, Herbert R. *Listening Your Way to Management Success*. Glenview, IL: Scott Foresman, 1983. 112p.

This is a concise, problem-solving look at listening skills. There are guidelines and suggestions for managers on improving both individual and group interactions. Indexed.

928. Lewis, Phillip V. *Organizational Communication: The Essence of Effective Management*. 3d ed. New York: John Wiley and Sons, 1987. 345p.

As a basic textbook in organizational communication, it places listening and interviewing in an organizational context. There are some guidelines. The appendices study writing letters and reports, and handling employment and exit interviews. Indexed.

929. Montgomery, Robert L. *Listening Made Easy*. Illustrated by Ric Estrada. New York: AMACOM, 1981. 134p.

After a discussion of the importance of listening, rules and principles are given for increasing listening ability. The book briefly looks at problems, causes of listening behavior, skill building blocks and applying those skills. Not indexed.

930. Murphy, Kevin J. *Effective Listening. Hearing What People Say and Making It Work For You*. New York: Bantam Books, 1987. 179p.

Listening for effective management is reviewed. The book supplies tips, quizzes, exercises and numerous illustrative axioms. Part three elaborates on listening for interviewing, selecting and training employees. Not indexed.

931. Steil, Lyman K.; Barker, Larry L.; and Watson, Kittie W. *Effective Listening: Key to Your Success*. Reading, MA: Addison-Wesley, 1983. 155p.

Based on training seminars conducted by the authors, listening improvement is emphasized through exercises and self-analysis tests. Key topics are improving awareness, understanding and developing listening excellence. There is a pre-test listening quiz. Indexed.

932. Steil, Lyman K.; Summerfield, Joanne; and de Mare, George. *Listening: It Can Change Your Life*. New York: John Wiley and Sons, 1983. 214p.

Interviews with twenty-five leaders are used to reveal the impact of listening in the past and today. Chapter five discusses techniques for improved listening. The appendix has an example of a personal listening profile. Indexed.

933. Wolf, Florence I., et al. *Perceptive Listening*. New York: Holt, Rinehart and Winston, 1983. 264p.

The college or business training textbook combines current listening theory with research-based principles. Chapter eight discloses seven productive techniques and chapter ten describes how listening affects business. Chapters have exercises and a bibliography. Indexed.

MEDIA RELATIONS

934. Hannaford, Peter. *Talking Back to the Media*. New York: Facts on File, 1986. 184p.

This well-researched book communicates the historical context in which the media has developed. Part two furnishes practical advice on dealing with the media. There are examples of specific situations. Indexed.

935. Robinson, James W. *Winning Them Over*. Rocklin, CA: Prima Publishing and Communications, 1987. 287p.

The ten strategies here demonstrate how to deal successfully with the media. The strategies employ ten steps in preparing and delivering speeches. Besides the advice offered, there are examples and a sample speech in the appendix. Indexed.

936. Thrash, Artie A.; Shelby, Annette N.; and Tarver, Jerry L. *Speaking Up Successfully*. New York: Holt, Rinehart and Winston, 1984. 248p.

Principles and strategies of business and professional communication are given in a textbook format. The authors provide advice and some samples for skill development in listening, interviews, meetings, media relations and presentations. The appendix explains parliamentary procedures. Indexed.

MEETINGS

937. Andrews, Patricia H., and Baird, John E. Jr. *Communication for Business and the Professions*. 3d ed. Dubuque, IA: Wm. C. Brown, 1986. 462p.

Oral communication activities deliberated in this textbook are meetings, interviews and presentations. There are numerous examples. Indexed.

938. Callanan, Joseph A. *Communicating: How to Organize Meetings and Presentations*. New York: Franklin Watts, 1984. 252p.

Techniques for improving performance in meetings and for delivering presentations are presented. Aimed at improving the skills of managers, the author unveils checklists, tips and outlines. Tests, selected remarks for speeches and research options are part of the appendices. Indexed.

939. DeBernardis, Frank, and O'Connor, Frank. *Meetings: Manage the Meetings and You'll Manage the Company*. Illustrated by Gill Fox. New York: Richardson and Steirman, 1986. 87p.

The authors' view of meeting management focuses on skill development and practical advice. Many cartoons illustrate major points. The processes involved have been simplified in order to demystify the business meeting. Not indexed.

940. Falcione, Raymond L. *The Guide to Better Communication in Government Service*. In consultation with James G. Dalton. Glenview, IL: Scott Foresman, 1984. 132p.

Communication in government service is examined. The goal to be achieved is improvement of listening, performance appraisal, meetings and problem-solving skills. A useful introduction to the subject, the exercises and case studies appear in the appendices. Besides many examples, there is a ratings chart that can be used to launch a communications audit. Indexed.

941. Gordon, Myron. *How to Plan and Conduct a Successful Meeting*. New York: Sterling Publishing Company, 1985. 178p.

First published in 1981, meeting styles are analyzed and improvements suggested for both leaders and participants. Chapters seven, sixteen and twenty one explain the elements, shaping, and ending of a meeting. Many examples and a glossary are available. Indexed.

942. Guth, Chester K., and Shaw, Stanley S. *How to Put on Dynamic Meetings*. Reston, VA: Reston Publishing Company, 1980. 147p.

The authors look at planning and staging meetings with an emphasis on the oral and visual. The book has an abundance of illustrations, a glossary, and an appendix on producing visuals. Indexed.

943. Hon, David. *Meetings That Matter*. New York: John Wiley and Sons, 1980. 132p.

The self-teaching guide for managers concerns productive and controllable task-oriented meetings. The workbook format has guidelines, checklists and application exercises. Indexed.

944. *How to Run Better Business Meetings*. rev ed. New York: McGraw-Hill, 1987. 216p.

This is a revised version of the 1979 book by B. Y. Auger. Designed as a guide to planning, formating and chairing business meetings, it designates rules, techniques, checklists, guidelines and sample forms. The chapters on visuals are excellent. Indexed.

945. Jones, Martin. *How to Organize Meetings*. New York: Beaufort Books, 1981. 138p.

The author guides part-time planners through five types of meetings. In clear, simple language plananers are offered checklists, step-by-step instructions, advice with some examples. The checklist for meetings appears in chapter one, the one for the budget in chapter three. Not indexed.

946. Kieffer, George D. *The Strategy of Meetings*. New York: Simon and Schuster, 1988. 318p.

Here are strategies and tips for leading and participating in meetings. The book stresses advancing both the organization and an individual's career. There are examples and a meeting checklist. Other skill areas studied are agendas, listening, and the rules of order. Indexed.

947. Kirkpatrick, Donald L. *How to Plan and Conduct Productive Business Meetings*. 2d ed. New York: AMACOM, 1987. 293p.

Different kinds of meetings, such as sales, in-house and departmental, are planned and conducted with this book. Causes of bad meetings and their solutions are reported. While most of the manual covers guidelines for meeting leaders, one chapter features participant preparation. The appendices contain a pre-test, post-test and materials for conducting a seminar. Indexed.

948. McCabe, Margaret E., and Rhoades, Jacqueline. *Cooperative Meeting Management: Stop Wasting Your Time*. Willits, CA: ITA Publication, 1986. 40p.

Volume unavailable for examination.

949. Mosvick, Roger K., and Nelson, Robert B. *We've Got to Start Meeting Like This! A Guide to Successful Business Meeting Management*. Glenview, IL: Scott Foresman, 1987. 258p.

After describing the results of a survey of managers, the authors elaborate on the techniques for more effective meetings. Although the book highlights the research results, chapter five and appendix A display guidelines for the planning and conducting of several different kinds of meetings. Indexed.

950. Newman, Pamela J., and Lynch, Alfred F. *Behind Closed Doors: A Guide to Successful Meetings*. Englewood Cliffs, NJ: Prentice-Hall, 1983. 189p.

The book is a basic guide to organizing and conducting meetings. While the emphasis is on groups of six to eight people, the principles can be applied to larger groups and to one-on-one situations, for example performance appraisals. The guidelines, checklists and forms are listed separately. Not indexed.

951. O'Connor, Rochelle. *Company Planning Meetings*. New York: The Conference Board, 1980. 50p.

As part of Conference Board Report Number 781, typical types of meetings are discussed. The exhibits supply sample agendas, review forms, and other documents useful for company planning meetings. Not indexed.

952. Palmer, Barbara C., and Palmer, Kenneth R. *The Successful Meeting Master Guide for Business and Professional People*. Englewood Cliffs, NJ: Prentice-Hall, 1983. 277p.

Simple methods for avoiding unnecessary meetings and for making necessary ones more effective are demonstrated. After describing the content found in a good meeting, the authors present advice on achieving excellence. There are examples of meeting checklists, schedules, agendas and other planning documents. Indexed.

953. Renton, Michael. *Getting Better Results from the Meetings You Run*. Champaign, IL: Research Press, 1980. 95p.

A self-help mode is used to explain discussion-leading and group problem-solving meetings. The self-test measures a readers understanding of the book's content. The case study followed throughout the book illustrates the short cuts presented. Not indexed.

954. Roberts, Dennis. *The Administration of Company Meetings*. Cambridge: ICSA Publishing, 1986. 136p.

This work explains how to run an annual, board or shareholders meeting. The checklists, drafts and other specimens are in the thirteen appendices. Focused on business in the United Kingdom, the book is most valuable for those doing business there. Indexed.

955. Uris, Auren. *The Executive Deskbook*. 3d ed. New York: Van Nostrand Reinhold, 1988. 427p.

The handbook, for management executives, provides guidelines, advice and tips in problem solving. The communications section explains how to choose a communications method and write a memo (with example). One chapter is devoted to meetings. There is a section of sample management forms. Indexed.

956. Ward, Sue. *A-Z of Meetings*. London: Pluto Press, 1985. 214p.

The rules and procedures of meetings are conveyed first. Then the author suggests ideas for running effective meetings. Designed for those holding formal meetings in Great Britain, there are checklists and examples. Meetingspeak and etiquette are covered in the appendices. Indexed.

957. Wood, Julia T.; Phillips, Gerald M.; and Pedersen, Douglas J. *Group Discussion: A Practical Guide to Participation and Leadership*. 2d ed. New York: Harper and Row, 1986. 218p.

A problem-solving method is employed in leading and participating in group discussions. Applicable for different size groups, the book advances theory, applications and guidelines. It considers the preparation of the final committee report and the oral presentation. Indexed.

PRESENTATIONS

958. Applbaum, Ronald L., and Anatol, Karl W. E. *Effective Oral Communication for Business and the Professions*. Chicago: Science Research Associates, 1982. 418p.

The skill development guidelines reveal recommendations and examples for more effective presentations, group discussions and interviews in the work environment. Chapters have exercises and case studies. Indexed.

959. Blumenthal, Lassor A. *Successful Oral and Written Presentations*. New York: Perigee Books, Putnam Publishing Company, 1987. 94p.

Preparing and delivering a successful presentation is stressed with examples. Two chapters concentrate on conferences and seminars. Indexed.

960. Dellinger, Susan, and Deane, Barbara. *Communicating Effectively: A Complete Guide for Better Managing*. Radnor, PA: Chilton Book Company, 1982. 251p.

Oral communication skills for managers are featured, particularly listening, interviewing, meeting and presentation skills. One chapter is devoted to writing skills. There are do's and don'ts, checklists, examples and exercises. The 1982 edition, a paperback version of the 1980 publication, was reprinted in 1987. Indexed.

961. Doolittle, Robert J. *Professionally Speaking: A Concise Guide*. Glenview, IL: Scott Foresman, 1984. 134p.

The author's method for delivering written material approaches the preparation, presention and evaluation systematically. The book also handles question and answer sessions. Indexed.

962. Fernandez, Thomas L. *Oral Communication for Business*. Reston, VA: Reston Publishing Company, 1984. 58p.

While discussing communication theory, the author advances tips for speeches and presentations. Frequently asked questions and two sample plans can be found in the appendices. Not indexed.

963. Fletcher, Leon. *Speaking to Succeed: In Business, Industry, Professions*. New York: Harper and Row, 1988. 329p.

This textbook, for students preparing for business and professional careers, concentrates on the improvement of speaking and other oral skills. Chapters have objectives, checklists, discussion suggestions and examples. Chapter eleven illustrates the use of computers and word processing in preparing speeches. The book fosters improvement of listening, meetings and presentations. The recommended reading at the end of the chapters analyzes the content of the two or three most relevant books. Indexed.

964. Frank, Allan D. *Communicating on the Job*. Glenview, IL: Scott Foresman, 1982. 344p.

The development of both general communication and specific oral skills is the concern of this textbook. It underscores the importance of organizational communication and interpersonal skills in listening, interviews and presentations. Indexed.

965. Goodall, H. Lloyd Jr., and Waagen, Christopher L. *The Persuasive Presentation. A Practical Guide to Professional Communication in Organizations*. New York: Harper and Row, 1986. 192p.

A case study is used to examine presentations in an organizational setting. Outlining appears in chapter three, sample presentations in chapters nine and ten. While designed for students, the emphasis on presentational settings in business and government enhances the relevancy of this book. Indexed.

966. Goodworth, Clive T. *Effective Speaking and Presentation for the Company Executive*. London: Business Books, 1980. 204p.

Presentations and the speaking roles of managers are portrayed humorously. Examples demonstrate what to do and what not to do. There are self-tutorial exercises in each chapter. While the book speaks from a British viewpoint, the content is relevant in any context. There is an appendix on legal proceedings. Indexed.

967. Griffin, C. W. *Writing: A Guide for Business Professionals*. New York: Harcourt Brace Jovanovich, 1987. 419p.

The author focuses on communication at work through examples of documents and realistic work situations. Writing techniques are applied to the writing of letters, memos, reports, proposals and manuals. Readers are shown how to prepare and deliver an oral presentation. There is a section on writing style and the use of editing. Troublesome words are listed at the back of the book. Indexed.

968. Henry, Lauchland A. *The Professional's Guide to Working Smarter.* Tenafly, NJ: Burrill-Ellsworth Associates, 1988. 208p.

Career management for professionals necessitates the ability to communicate effectively. The author displays suggestions and general guidelines for report writing, meetings and presentations. The appendices have tips for speaking, listening, reading, presentations and meetings. Indexed.

969. Holcombe, Marya W., and Stein, Judith K. *Presentations for Decision Makers.* New York: Van Nostrand Reinhold, 1983. 216p.

The authors disclose their system for developing and delivering an oral presentation. It can be used for meetings, videoconferences, and speaking outside an organization. Guidelines, checklists and numerous examples are provided. Not indexed.

970. Howell, William S., and Bormann, Ernest G. *The Process of Presentational Speaking.* 2d ed. New York: Harper and Row, 1988. 223p.

Principles, directions and procedures are given for preparing effective presentations. The how-to approach stresses guidelines and techniques. There is a chapter on listening skills. Chapters include a review and discussion questions. The appendix has six case studies. Indexed.

971. Lambert, Clark. *The Business Presentations Workbook.* Englewood Cliffs, NJ: Prentice-Hall, 1988. 223p.

Volume unavailable for examination.

972. Leech, Thomas. *How to Prepare, Stage, and Deliver Winning Presentations.* New York: AMACOM, 1982. 417p.

The book advances a systems approach for planning, designing and delivering a presentation individually or as part of a team. The book, which has advice, examples and a glossary, can also be used as handbook. Indexed.

973. LeRoux, Paul. *Selling to a Group: Presentation Strategies.* New York: Barnes and Noble, 1984. 163p.

Strategies and tips in this volume support the presentation of ideas, products or services to a group. There are specific tips for improving performance and outcome, with many examples. Parts of the book can be used in other types of presentations. Indexed.

974. Linver, Sandy, and Taylor, Nick. *Speak and Get Results. The Complete Guide to Speeches and Presentations That Work in Any Business Situation.* New York: Summit Books, 1983. 286p.

Creating effective presentations is the intention of this volume. The authors offer no short cuts but do explain the reasons for careful planning and execution. The table of contents for part one can function as an outline of the preparation process. Chapter twelve contains pointers on special situations such as teleconferencing, addressing the media, and large meetings. Not indexed.

975. Mercer, Michael W. *How Winners Do It: High Impact People Skills for Your Career Success.* Winnetka, IL: Wellington Publishers, 1988. 224p.

The author's view of career development emphasizes people-oriented skills. The discussion of rapport and negotiating skills is followed by chapters on presentations, meetings and basic writing skills. The book examines learnable skills with examples, illustrations, and case studies in chapter eight. A sample presentation (both text and transparencies) is in the appendix. Indexed.

976. Meuse, Leonard F. Jr. *Mastering the Business and Technical Presentation.* Boston: CBI Publishing Company, 1980. 123p

This manual is comprised of preparation and delivery techniques for audiovisual presentations. The five-step process uses suggestions, tips, tactics and checklists which were drawn from the author's experience. Not indexed.

977. Meuse, Leonard F. Jr. *Succeeding at Business and Technical Presentations.* 2d ed. New York: John Wiley and Sons, 1988. 192p.

A second and expanded edition of the author's 1980 work, the book emphasizes the best way to prepare a presentation and describes the most useful delivery techniques. There are guidelines, checklists and many examples. Use of visual aids to enhance a presentation is related. There is a separate list of the illustrations. Indexed.

978. Parkhurst, William. *The Eloquent Executive. A Guide to High-Impact Speaking in Big Meetings, Small Meetings, and One-on-One.* New York: Times Books, 1988. 128p.

The volume consists of a compilation of strategies and advice for executives and managers. The book goes beyond platform speaking in handling meetings and social occasions. Chapter four shows how to write a presentation in a half hour. Question and answer sessions, voice control and other related issues are reported. Not indexed.

979. Peoples, David A. *Presentations Plus.* New York: John Wiley and Sons, 1988. 239p.

The author elaborates on his method, the blueprint for success, for developing and delivering a presentation. The method employs tips and techniques for writing, illustrating and answering questions. Indexed.

980. Richards, Ian. *How to Give a Successful Presentation. A Concise Guide for Every Manager.* London: Graham and Trotman, 1988. 90p.

The book guides managers through the stages of preparing and delivering oral presentations. Chapters debate the advantages and disadvantages of different methods. The author considers planning, making visual aids, picking visuals, and presenting yourself effectively. There are many illustrations. Indexed.

981. Seiler, William J.; Baudhuin, E. Scott; and Schuelke, L. David. *Communication in Business and Professional Organizations.* Reading, MA: Addison-Wesley, 1982. 351p.

The application and skill sections of this organizational communications textbook examine listening, interviewing and oral presentations in some depth. There are examples and discussion questions. Additional readings are listed in each chapter, a glossary at the back of the book. Indexed.

982. Smith, Terry C. *Making Successful Presentations: A Self-Teaching Guide*. New York: John Wiley and Sons, 1984. 182p.

A sequence is suggested for planning, organizing, developing and delivering a presentation. The book has checklists and an emergency kit. Indexed.

983. Thomas, David A., and Fryar, Maridell. *Successful Business Speaking*. Skokie, IL: National Textbook Company, 1981. 91p.

Part one reports on recent research in business communication. Parts two and three supply guidelines and sample outlines for preparing and delivering presentations within an organization and outside it. Indexed.

984. Timm, Paul R. *Functional Business Presentations: Getting Across*. Englewood Cliffs, NJ: Prentice-Hall, 1981. 206p.

This textbook contains guidance and practice in preparing and delivering oral presentations. Checklists, worksheets and a critique form are in the appendix. Indexed.

985. Vardaman, George T. *Making Successful Presentations*. New York: AMACOM, 1980. 271p.

The author explains his method (TRIM) for creating oral and written presentations. For managers, the book reviews principles and reprints twenty presentations as examples. Indexed.

PUBLIC SPEAKING

986. Baird, John E. Jr. *Speaking for Results: Communication by Objectives*. New York: Harper and Row, 1981. 301p.

Speeches are developed and presented through the establishment of objectives. The book is organized according to the three key steps in public speaking that have been identified by the author. Projects and a sample speech in the appendix. Indexed.

987. Bell, Arthur H., and Skopec, Eric W. *The Speaker's Edge. Tips for Confident Presenting*. Westbury, NY: Asher-Gallant Press, 1988. 139p.

An easy approach to public speaking is suggested with tips, checklists and blank worksheets. The book is concerned with the planning and organization of the presentation, and with the polishing of delivery skills. The book has a chapter on coaching others, a list of forms and a list of figures. Not indexed.

988. Bormann, Ernest G., and Bormann, Nancy C. *Speech Communication: A Basic Approach*. 3d ed. New York: Harper and Row, 1981. 278p.

A basic text for a course in public speaking or small group communication, the book has been revised to incorporate a more practical approach. The chapters on preparing and delivering speeches supply key ideas and examples. Indexed.

989. Capps, Randall; Dodd, Carley H.; and Winn, Larry J. *Communication for the Business and Professional Speaker*. New York: Macmillan; London: Collier Macmillan, 1981. 300p.

The theory and techniques of public speaking are investigated in a textbook. Arranged in five self-contained units, the book acquaints readers with interviewing, meetings, conferences, public speaking and listening. Sample speeches appear in the appendix. Indexed.

990. Detz, Joan. *How to Write and Give A Speech.* New York: St. Martin's Press, 1984. 143p.

Speech preparation for executives and managers is examined. Chapter nine, on special-occasion speeches, describes introducing speakers, panel presentations and handling question and answer sessions. Indexed.

991. Dutton, John L. *How to Be an Outstanding Speaker: Eight Separate Secrets.* New London, WI: Life Skills Publishing, 1986. 232p.

Volume unavailable for examination.

992. Grice, George L., and Jones, M. Anway, eds. *Business and Professional Communication: Selected Readings.* Dubuque, IA: Kendall/Hunt Publishing, 1986. 123p.

A collection of twenty-three readings, the book is designed to bridge the gap between classroom concepts and business practice. While not comprehensive in its coverage of business communication, public speaking and the employment interview are discussed at some length. Not indexed.

993. Gronbeck, Bruce E. *The Articulate Person.* 2d ed. Glenview, IL: Scott Foresman, 1983. 294p.

While basically a textbook on the principles and applications of public speaking, the applications section provides practical tips, examples, and samples of different kinds of speeches. The book contains speeches for celebrating occasions. Models can be located through the table of contents. Indexed.

994. Holm, James N. Jr. *Productive Speech Communication for Business and the Professions.* Boston: American Press, 1985. 495p.

Volume unavailable for examination.

995. Humes, James C. *Talk Your Way to the Top.* New York: McGraw-Hill, 1980. 170p.

How to communicate effectively is revealed with humorous examples from the author's experience as a speech writer. The book is limited primarily to public speaking situations such as speeches, conferences, meetings and the telephone. Not indexed.

996. Kenny, Michael. *Presenting Yourself.* New York: John Wiley and Sons, 1982. 175p.

Produced for the Eastman Kodak Company, this how-to book provides guidelines and checklists on the preparation of a speech. Its focus is on visuals with many colorful illustrations. Indexed.

997. Kenny, Peter. *A Handbook of Public Speaking for Scientists and Engineers.* Bristol, UK: Adam Hilger, 1982. 181p.

The concise handbook, for the preparation of conference speeches, is concerned with skill development. Preparation and presentation are communicated with examples. Part two discusses meetings. Checklists, evaluation checklists and examinations are in the appendices. Indexed.

998. Koehler, Jerry W. and Sisco, John I. *Public Communication in Business and the Professions.* St. Paul, MN: West Publishing Company, 1981. 215p.

Concerned with the dissemination of information, the authors investigate presentations, conference speeches, listening skills and interviews. Sample speeches and evaluation techniques are in chapter fourteen. Indexed.

999. Martel, Myles. *Before You Say a Word: The Executive Guide to Effective Communication.* Englewood Cliffs, NJ: Prentice-Hall, 1984. 215p.

The principles of oral communication are applied to presentations, speeches, meetings, listening and dealing with the media. Executives are given a specific system for developing and disseminating goal-oriented messages. The text has examples, guidelines and a case study. Indexed.

1000. Powell, J. Lewis. *Executive Speaking: An Acquired Skill.* 2d ed. Washington, DC: Bureau of National Affairs, 1980. 163p.

The author promotes the effective speaking of executives. The how-to book has examples and cartoon illustrations. Although the chapter headings are confusing, the book is very practical in its focus. Chapter twelve delineates the basic speaker's checklist. Indexed.

1001. Rodman, George. *Public Speaking.* 3d ed. New York: Holt, Rinehart and Winston, 1986. 311p.

The public speaking textbook demonstrates guidelines for outlining and preparing a speech. There are sample speeches. Chapter thirteen considers speaking on radio and television. Indexed.

1002. Samovar, Larry A.; King, Stephen W.; and Lustig, Myron W. *Speech Communication in Business and the Professions.* Belmont, CA: Wadsworth Publishing Company 1981. 244p.

Principles and techniques are reviewed for the development of oral communication skills. The authors examine public speaking, group discussions and interviewing. Indexed.

1003. Scott, Bill. *The Skills of Communicating.* New York: Nichols Publishing Company, 1986. 198p.

For managers, communication techniques and skills are outlined for speaking, writing letters and reports, attending and leading meetings, and interviewing. There are some illustrations. Not indexed.

1004. Tacey, William S. *Business and Professional Speaking.* 4th ed. Dubuque, IA: Wm. C. Brown, 1983. 280p.

The textbook highlights public speaking in business and professional settings. The author answers queries with regard to preparing and delivering speeches, conducting interviews and listening. The appendix has sample speeches for analysis and study. Indexed.

1005. VanOosting, James. *The Business Speech: Speaker, Audience, and Text.* Englewood Cliffs, NJ: Prentice-Hall, 1985. 264p.

The theory and practice of business public speaking are cited. Chapters fifteen through twenty-two disclose guidelines, examples, exercises, models of specific types of speeches and blank forms for critiquing speeches. Indexed.

QUESTION AND ANSWER SESSIONS

1006. Berko, Roy M.; Wolvin, Andrew D.; and Curtis, Ray. *This Business of Communicating.* Dubuque, IA: Wm. C. Brown, 1986. 335p.

Primarily about organizational communication, the book reinforces advice with many real examples. The examples demonstrate interviewing, public speaking and handling question-answer sessions. The sample outlines can be located in the table of contents. Indexed.

1007. Martel, Myles. *Mastering the Art of Q & A: A Survival Guide for Tough, Trick, and Hostile Questions.* Homewood, IL: Dow Jones-Irwin, 1989. 217p.

This is a practical guide to question and answer situations in the business environment. The author points out the importance of credibility and control in quality questioning. Part five has practical guidelines for several situations: questions after a speech, a news conference, TV interviews, talk shows, job interviews and testifying before government agencies. Indexed.

SPEAKING

1008. Hamlin, Sonya. *How to Talk so People Listen: The Real Key to Job Success.* New York: Harper and Row, 1988. 265p.

Volume unavailable for examination.

1009. Micali, Paul J. *How to Talk Your Way to Success.* rev ed. New York: E.P. Dutton, 1983. 142p.

Lessons are featured for improving speaking skills, removing bad habits, increasing vocabulary, releasing tension and creating an impact. The book briefly considers meetings and presentations. Not indexed.

1010. Skopec, Eric W. *Business and Professional Speaking.* Englewood Cliffs, NJ: Prentice-Hall, 1983. 266p.

Presentational speaking skills are introduced for four organizational situations. The textbook studies speaking in dyads, meetings and interviews. Cartoons and other illustrations are used to demonstrate the author's points. Indexed.

1011. Solomon, Muriel. *What Do I Say When -- A Guidebook for Getting Your Way with People on the Job.* Englewood Cliffs, NJ: Prentice-Hall, 1988. 296p.

Volume unavailable for examination.

1012. Turk, Christopher. *Effective Speaking: Communicating in Speech.* London: E. and F. N. Spon, 1985. 275p.

Those who must speak as part of the jobs can use this book to improve their speaking skills. The author reviews the presentation, the physical environment and answering questions. There are practice exercises. Indexed.

1013. Wilder, Lilyan. *Professionally Speaking.* New York: Simon and Schuster, 1986. 320p.

The author presents her four-step program for improving the voice and speaking in business situations. Areas considered are interviews, media relations with television and radio, and meetings. Indexed.

TELEPHONE SKILLS

1014. Cool, Lisa C. *How to Give Good Phone. Telephone Techniques to Increase Your Power, Profits and Performance.* New York: Donald I. Fine, 1988. 222p.

This is a guide to the techniques and strategies of effective telephone usage. While the emphasis is on profitability and selling, effective listening skills, techniques and tips for a more powerful telephone personality are provided. There is an excellent section on telephone equipment availability and usage. Not indexed.

1015. Frank, Milo O. *How to Get Your Point Across in 30 Seconds -- Or Less.* New York: Simon and Schuster, 1986. 120p.

The author contends that persuasive communication will bring results in thirty seconds. The key objectives and elements of messages are identified with examples. Chapter eleven recounts specific encounters with the telephone and answering machines. Memos, letters and notes are briefly discussed. The book is best used by those who already have some grounding in basic communication skills. Not indexed.

1016. Jackson, Dale E. *Interpersonal Communication for Technically Trained Managers. A Guide to Skills and Techniques.* New York: Quorum Books, 1988. 173p.

Designed for the improvement of managerial communication skills, the author supplies examples, guidelines and problem-solving exercises. The problem-solving nature of interpersonal communication skills is shown with chapters on listening, meetings and telephone skills. There is a brief glossary of communication terms. Indexed.

1017. Slaughter, Audrey. *Getting Through: How to Get the Better of the Telephone.* London: New English Library, 1981. 128p.

Volume unavailable for examination.

1018. Thomas, David A., and Fryar, Maridell. *Business Communication Today.* 2d ed. Lincolnwood, IL: National Textbook Company, 1988. 532p.

The second edition of this business communication textbook has more material on written skills. The book fosters skill development for listening, presentations, telephone usage, interviewing, the resume, letters, memos and other written forms. Examples are provided of letters, memos and press releases. The end of chapter reviews can be used as checklists. There is a handbook of grammar, punctuation and usage. Indexed.

1019. Weiss, Donald. *Winning on the Telephone*. New York: American Management Association, 1988. 57p.

Using the telephone in business is the focus here. Individual chapters offer tips on effective listening, getting your message across and handling problem callers. Indexed.

TELEVISION INTERVIEWING

1020. Blythin, Evan, and Samovar, Larry A. *Communicating Effectively on Television*. Belmont, CA: Wadsworth Publishing Company, 1985. 220p.

Designed for professionals who must appear on television, the authors reveal how to develop an appropriate message, present oneself, and prepare for the television interview. The work is organized around the sequence of events routinely found in television interviews. There are introductions to the television studio and to the most common form of television presentation. Chapters include recommended readings and an evaluation form. Indexed.

1021. Valenti, Jack. *Speak Up with Confidence. How to Prepare, Lean, and Deliver Effective Speeches*. New York: William Morrow, 1982. 152p.

The author's simple rules emphasize thinking and practice in improving presentation skills. The rules, told with humor, encourage the use of discipline in achieving professionalism. How to speak before television cameras is also considered. Not indexed.

WORKSHOPS AND SEMINARS

1022. Cooper, Susan, and Heenan, Cathy. *Preparing, Designing, and Leading Workshops: A Humanistic Approach*. New York: Van Nostrand Reinhold, 1984. 138p.

A practical model is given for planning and running a seminar or workshop. Checklists and sample forms are in the appendices. Not indexed.

1023. Murray, Sheila L. *How to Organize and Manage a -- Seminar.* Englewood Cliffs, NJ: Prentice-Hall, 1983. 204p.

This manual elaborates on the staging and logistics of seminars, workshops and conferences. The chronological approach examines the key areas with examples. Addresses of speakers bureaus and associations are given. Indexed.

1024. Schindler-Rainman, Eva. *Taking Your Meetings Out of the Doldrums*. rev ed. In collaboration with Jack Cole. San Diego, CA: University Associates, 1988. 123p.

This book is concerned with designing, planning and leading meetings, seminars, workshops and other learning activities. In nine units, the author unveils guidelines, tips, checklists and blank worksheets that can be adapted as needed. There are sample checklists, and evaluation forms. Not indexed.

NAME INDEX

TITLE INDEX

[Numbers given refer to item numbers.]

SUBJECT INDEX

About the Compiler

SANDRA E. BELANGER is an Associate Librarian, Reference, at San Jose State University. Her articles have appeared in *Journal of Library History, Business Woman, CMLEA Journal, Online Review,* and *Journal of Academic Librarianship.*